A WRITER REFORMS (THE TEACHING OF) WRITING: DONALD MURRAY AND THE WRITING PROCESS MOVEMENT, 1963–1987

PERSPECTIVES ON WRITING

Series Editors: Rich Rice, Heather MacNeill Falconer, and J. Michael Rifenburg
Consulting Editor: Susan H. McLeod | Associate Editor: Olivia Johnson

The Perspectives on Writing series addresses writing studies in a broad sense. Consistent with the wide ranging approaches characteristic of teaching and scholarship in writing across the curriculum, the series presents works that take divergent perspectives on working as a writer, teaching writing, administering writing programs, and studying writing in its various forms.

The WAC Clearinghouse and University Press of Colorado are collaborating so that these books will be widely available through free digital distribution and low-cost print editions. The publishers and the series editors are committed to the principle that knowledge should freely circulate and have embraced the use of technology to support open access to scholarly work.

Recent Books in the Series

Michelle LaFrance and Melissa Nicolas (Eds.), *Institutional Ethnography as Writing Studies Practice* (2023)

Phoebe Jackson and Christopher Weaver (Eds.), *Rethinking Peer Review: Critical Reflections on a Pedagogical Practice* (2023)

Megan J. Kelly, Heather M. Falconer, Caleb L. González, and Jill Dahlman (Eds.), *Adapting the Past to Reimagine Possible Futures: Celebrating and Critiquing WAC at 50* (2023)

William J. Macauley, Jr. et al. (Eds.), *Threshold Conscripts: Rhetoric and Composition Teaching Assistantships* (2023)

Jennifer Grouling, *Adapting VALUEs: Tracing the Life of a Rubric through Institutional Ethnography* (2022)

Chris M. Anson and Pamela Flash (Eds.), *Writing-Enriched Curricula: Models of Faculty-Driven and Departmental Transformation* (2021)

Asao B. Inoue, *Above the Well: An Antiracist Argument From a Boy of Color* (2021)

Alexandria L. Lockett, Iris D. Ruiz, James Chase Sanchez, and Christopher Carter (Eds.), *Race, Rhetoric, and Research Methods* (2021)

Kristopher M. Lotier, *Postprocess Postmortem* (2021)

Ryan J. Dippre and Talinn Phillips (Eds.), *Approaches to Lifespan Writing Research: Generating an Actionable Coherence* (2020)

Lesley Erin Bartlett, Sandra L. Tarabochia, Andrea R. Olinger, and Margaret J. Marshall (Eds.), *Diverse Approaches to Teaching, Learning, and Writing Across the Curriculum: IWAC at 25* (2020)

Hannah J. Rule, *Situating Writing Processes* (2019)

A WRITER REFORMS (THE TEACHING OF) WRITING: DONALD MURRAY AND THE WRITING PROCESS MOVEMENT, 1963–1987

Michael J. Michaud

The WAC Clearinghouse
wac.colostate.edu
Fort Collins, Colorado

University Press of Colorado
upcolorado.com
Denver, Colorado

The WAC Clearinghouse, Fort Collins, Colorado 80523

University Press of Colorado, Denver, Colorado 80202

ISBN 978-1-64215-204-3 (PDF) | 978-1-64215-205-0 (ePub) | 978-1-64642-573-0 (pbk.)

DOI 10.37514/PER-B.2023.2043

Produced in the United States of America

Library of Congress Cataloging-in-Publication Data

Names: Michaud, Michael J., 1973– author.
Title: A writer reforms (the teaching of) writing : Donald Murray and the writing process
  movement, 1963–1987 / Michael J. Michaud.
Other titles: Writer reforms the teaching of writing
Description: Fort Collins, Colorado : The WAC Clearinghouse ; Denver, Colorado : University
  Press of Colorado, 2023. | Series: Perspectives on writing | Includes bibliographical references.
Identifiers: LCCN 2023039423 (print) | LCCN 2023039424 (ebook) | ISBN 9781646425730
  (paperback) | ISBN 9781642152043 (adobe pdf) | ISBN 9781642152050 (epub)
Subjects: LCSH: Murray, Donald M. (Donald Morison), 1924–2006. | College teachers—
  New Hampshire—Biography. | English teachers—New Hampshire—Biography. | English
  language—Rhetoric—Study and teaching (Higher)—United States. | Report writing—Study
  and teaching (Higher)—United States. | LCGFT: Biographies.
Classification: LCC PE64.M79 M53 2023 (print) | LCC PE64.M79 (ebook) | DDC
  808/.042092 [B]—dc23/eng/20231011
LC record available at https://lccn.loc.gov/2023039423
LC ebook record available at https://lccn.loc.gov/2023039424

Copyeditor: Don Donahue
Designer: Mike Palmquist
Cover Photos: Donald Murray Collection. Courtesy of the Milne Special Collections and
  Archives, University of New Hampshire.
Series Editors: Rich Rice, Heather MacNeill Falconer, and J. Michael Rifenburg
Consulting Editor: Susan H. McLeod

The WAC Clearinghouse supports teachers of writing across the disciplines. Hosted by Colorado
State University, it brings together scholarly journals and book series as well as resources for
teachers who use writing in their courses. This book is available in digital formats for free
download at wac.colostate.edu.

Founded in 1965, the University Press of Colorado is a nonprofit cooperative publishing enterprise
supported, in part, by Adams State University, Colorado State University, Fort Lewis College,
Metropolitan State University of Denver, University of Alaska Fairbanks, University of Colorado,
University of Denver, University of Northern Colorado, University of Wyoming, Utah State
University, and Western Colorado University. For more information, visit upcolorado.com.

Land Acknowledgment. The Colorado State University Land Acknowledgment can be found at
landacknowledgment.colostate.edu.

To the members of my UNH writing "tribe,"
who have taught, nurtured, shaped, and cheered me.

CONTENTS

ACKNOWLEDGMENTS

In a lovely remembrance of her time at the University of New Hampshire (UNH) in the 1980s, "A Stand in Time and Place: New Hampshire and the Teaching of Writing," Bonnie Sunstein writes, "Once in a while we get lucky—time and space and context converge to encircle a community of like-minded people to encourage, voices in counterpoint and harmony, giving birth to a rich and productive intellectual moment that helps to shape a profession" (121). I arrived at UNH in 1992, at the tail end of the period Sunstein describes in her essay, too late to be a part of it, but near enough to its conclusion to bask in its warm afterglow. As such, I would like to acknowledge the many UNHers who contributed to my growth and development as a teacher, scholar, writer and to this project.

First among these is Donald Murray, himself, who welcomed me into his home in the late summer of 1996 to discuss writing and teaching as I headed off to pursue a masters degree under Sunstein's tutelage at the University of Iowa. Seven years later, now a student in the doctoral program in English composition at UNH, I interviewed Murray for a paper I was writing for a course on the history of the field. While I did not know him as Sunstein and other members of her generation did, Murray was generous with me and always happy to talk writing and teaching and encourage my pursuits. I have tried to imagine how he would feel, were he still alive, to know that I have gone on to write a book about him. I can only hope that he would recognize himself in it and feel that I have fairly and accurately conveyed not just an accounting of his work and accomplishments in the field, but also a sense of his large and generous spirit.

The list of additional UNHers I would like to acknowledge here is long and distinguished. Bonnie Sunstein, my first (and only) "Jewish Mother," served as my initial tour-guide to the UNH writing/teaching community. During my time at Iowa, Bonnie was planning a commemorative session for Murray at the 1997 NCTE conference and asked if, in my capacity as her research assistant, I would transcribe a series of interviews she had conducted with Murray. Beyond reading him in Bonnie's Approaches to Teaching Writing class that fall of 1997, listening to him and transcribing his words was my first opportunity to really get to know Murray, to learn of his personal story and of his work at UNH and in the field beyond. Many years later, while I was conducting research for this book, Bonnie generously shared documents from her personal archive with me and helped arrange interviews with former UNH faculty members and staff. Throughout my career, Bonnie has played an instrumental role in my development for which I am incredibly grateful.

Thomas Newkirk has been a significant mentor in my career and played an essential role in the writing and development of this book. Tom sat for multiple interviews, shared materials from his professional files and archive, consulted and read drafts at numerous moments in the writing and research process, and found and shared the video of Murray from the Iowa Writer's Conference that I draw on in the book's Preface. Since first working with Tom during my years as an adjunct English instructor at UNH, he has supported and encouraged me, playing the role of a generous reader and critic, colleague, and friend. This book could not have been written without his guidance, help, and support.

Other UNHers who have played a pivotal role in the writing of this book include Lad Tobin who, in an email written during the early years of this project, in response to a draft of an essay I had sent him about Murray, challenged me to think more carefully about why I wanted to write about Murray in the first place, thus setting in motion the process that ultimately led to this book. Lad's feedback proved to be the nudge I needed to get into Murray's archive to try to create what others had not, i.e., an historical accounting of Murray's contributions to the teaching and researching of writing at UNH and in the field of composition beyond.

Bruce Ballenger and Bronwyn Williams also played a critical part in the writing of this book. Each read multiple drafts of the manuscript, offered critical comments and perspectives, supplied developmental and editorial suggestions, and delivered much-needed praise, reassurance, and encouragement. Peter Elbow once claimed that the most valuable gift a writer can have is "not a critic or an evaluator but an audience" (8). Bruce and Bronwyn gave me the audience I needed repeatedly over the span of many years and for that I am grateful.

Additional members of the UNH community I would like to thank for their contributions to this project include Richard Goodman, Thomas Carnicelli, Lester Fisher, Brock Dethier, Lisa Miller, Andy Merton, Donna Qualley, Katherine Tirabassi, Robert J. Begiebing, J. Dennis Robinson, Ruth Clogston, Sue Wheeler, Rebecca Rule, Donald Silva, Paul Lewis, Robert Fried, Bill Childs, Richard Pevear, Peter Keville, Paul Roberge, Michael Lee, Russell Banks, H. Eric Branscomb, Christopher "Chip" Scanlon, and Sally Lentz. Special thanks go to UNH archivists Bill Ross and Elizabeth Slomba and especially to Mylinda Woodward, who guided and supported me through many years of visits to the Milne Special Collections and Archives at UNH. Added thanks go to current and past members of the UNH English Department professional staff, including Carla Cannizarro, Jennifer Dube, Sabina Foote, and Jeanine Auger.

Beyond the UNH family of writers, teachers, and scholars, there are many other people to thank for their support and help with this project. I would like to thank Rhode Island College and its Committee on Faculty Scholarship for travel funding and research support, as well as release time to write. I would like to thank Ruba Bouzan, now an alum of the RIC English graduate program, for transcribing interviews. Finally, I would like to thank my colleagues Carolyn Obel-Omia and Martha Horn for reading early drafts of this manuscript and offering feedback, encouragement, and support.

Beyond UNH and RIC, I would like to thank Doug Downs, D. Shane Combs, Jeremiah Dyehouse, Chris Anson, and Sarah Read for reading chapters of this book at various times and offering criticism and feedback. Thanks, also, to the anonymous reviewers at the WAC Clearinghouse for their insightful and supportive feedback and to my editors, Rich Rice, Heather Falconer, and Michael Rifenburg. Thanks, as well, go to Olivia Johnson, who generously offered editorial support on citation practices for archival documents. Finally, huge thanks go to Mike Palmquist, for believing in this project but also for his tireless advocacy on behalf of our field.

Additionally, I would like to thank David Shedden, formerly of the Poynter Institute (St. Petersburg, FL), for supporting this project early on with photocopies of documents from Murray's archive. I would like to thank my mother, Pat Michaud, who scanned and digitized thousands of pages of documents from Murray's archive. I would like to thank Bill and Barbara Newton for providing lodging and encouragement during my numerous trips to Durham, as well as childcare which freed me up to spend time in the archives. I would like to thank Hannah Starobin, Donald Murray's daughter, for her support of this book. I would also like to thank local friends who have inquired about the status of this project and encouraged me over many years: Michael Lynch, Ron Chofay, Jason Marsocci. And I would like to thank the anonymous donors who generously paid the freight to return Donald Murray's archive to UNH in 2017. Without their financial assistance, I would not have had access to Murray's materials, and this book would not have been written. I would like to thank the taxpayers and citizens of the states of New Hampshire, Iowa, and Rhode Island, the first two of whom supported my undergraduate and graduate education, the latter of whom pay my salary.

Thanks, finally, to my wife Shelagh and kids, William and Emma, for loving me and being the best support system I could ask for over the many years it has taken for me to bring this project to fruition.

PREFACE

The teachers come to the Holiday Inn of Iowa City, Iowa in October 1985 for the fall conference of the Iowa Writers Project.[1] They pack the hotel ballroom and wait with anticipation for the talk to begin. Onstage, at the podium, with thinning white hair and large black glasses, Donald Murray fumbles with his lapel microphone until his voice booms out over the room's PA system. Sixty-one years old and two-years away from retirement, Murray has been riding circuit, spreading the gospel of "writing process" to packed rooms of teachers since the mid 1960s. "My folks started me out in life to be a boy evangelist," he once mused in a sabbatical report. "I rejected that to find myself becoming a sort of educational evangelist" (Murray Sabbatical Report 1970).

As the audience quiets down and settles in, Murray extends comments made during his introduction about his wife, Minnie Mae, who assists him in his writing. "I would not be a writer without her," he says. "And that's something that I think is important to mention." He then tells a story about how Minnie Mae once mailed out his manuscripts when he thought they were no good and soon they were accepted and published, thus launching his freelance career. "So I really do owe everything to her," Murray says. "She's my best friend and with my writing she's all involved in it."

After a minute or so more of introductory comments, Murray gets down to business. He explains that his talk will begin with a series of dramatic performances in which he will play the part of a typical English teacher and Jim Davis, the Iowa Project's director, will play the part of a student. Together, Murray explains, they will present three brief sketches of writing conferences in order to dramatize what Murray calls a response-approach to composition pedagogy. When the dramatic element of the talk is over, Murray says, he will speak for a few minutes longer and then take questions. Having finished his preliminary comments Murray invites Davis to the stage and they begin.

In the first conference, Murray and Davis make small talk until Davis mentions that he sometimes likes to write poetry. Murray jumps at this and asks if Davis will share one of his poems. Davis says he will, but before he can begin reading Murray says, "Before you read it, I'd like to know what you think of it." Davis shrugs disinterestedly and says he is mostly pleased with the poem. Then he reads. When he's done Murray explodes with enthusiasm. "Oh, I like that!" he erupts, heaping praise on Davis. Would he (Davis) be willing to

---

1   The scene I describe here is drawn from a video of Murray's actual talk at the Iowa Writer's Project on October 13, 1985. Thank you to Thomas Newkirk for sharing the video with me.

share more poems at their next meeting, Murray asks. Davis says yes and the conference ends.

In the second conference, Davis shares another poem, this one unfinished. "What do you like about it?" Murray asks when Davis has finished reading it. Davis fumbles an answer and Murray listens attentively. Davis then asks Murray what he thinks of the poem, but Murray sidesteps the question and shares a story about an experience like the one Davis described in the poem. Davis persists, though, pressing Murray for a response. Murray defers but asks if he can get back to Davis with some thoughts at their next conference. Davis agrees. "What do you intend to do with the poem next?" Murray asks as they wrap up. Davis confesses he's unsure. "Do you mind if I mess with it a bit?" Murray says. Davis nods and the second conference ends.

In the third conference, Davis shares a final poem, one he has only just begun to write. When he's done reading it he again asks for Murray's impressions and this time Murray takes the bait. "In some of the conferences," he says, weighing his words carefully, "you're worried a little bit about whether people will understand you, but when we're first writing I think we try to tell people how to feel or worry about their feelings too much. You can't do that. You've got to just get right there and let me feel it and then see what happens. Follow your eye, follow your ear." Davis nods, pauses, and then says, "How do you become a poet?" "I guess you write poetry," Murray replies, not missing a beat, "which you're already doing." Davis smiles, thanks Murray, and says he will keep working. The third conference ends.

With the dramatic element of the program concluded, Davis returns to his seat and Murray takes his place at the podium once again. "What we've been doing here," he begins, "is response-teaching." He pauses a moment, takes a drink, and continues. "My preparation for this was my own writing this morning, and my writing other mornings, and my reading this morning. And some quiet time. And seeing some human beings. And being alive." Here, Murray pauses and then he continues. "There's no way I can prepare for a conference," he says. "I don't know what the students need to know. There is no content in the traditional sense. There's nothing that I feel I have to tell people. There's no absolute sequence of what they need. I take the student where the student is. Listen to the student. Listen to the text. Respond as a human being as best I can."

~~~

By October 1985 Donald Murray had been evangelizing to ballrooms of teachers like the one in Iowa City for just over twenty years. Having spent a lifetime studying the testimony of published writers and the first half of his career as a working writer, Murray was, by the standard of the day, well-qualified to speak on the topic of writing and its making. Having spent his Depression-era childhood and adolescence struggling to succeed in school and ultimately failing out, he was similarly qualified to speak on teaching and learning, education and schooling. During his second unanticipated career as a college English professor, Murray mobilized his curious ethos as a Pulitzer Prize-winning high school dropout to work to reform not just the teaching of writing in schools but schools *themselves*. No one was more surprised by this turn of events than Murray himself. "In a lifetime," he writes in his memoir *My Twice-Lived Life*, "I moved from being one of the dumb kids sitting in the back row, to standing behind the teacher's desk, to teaching teachers. I have, indeed, lived an unexpected life" (141).

~~~

Over the course of the decade or so that I have been at work on this project, investigating the unexpected life and work of one of composition and rhetoric's earliest and most prolific founders, I have learned that Donald Murray's personal backstory is at the center of his project of educational and disciplinary reform. Murray's is a uniquely twentieth-century American tale of class uplift and bootstrapping—a story of a difficult and complicated childhood in a working-class family south of Boston; of a quest to escape isolation and alienation at home, in the classroom, and on the playground; and of a project to remake oneself in war, college, and the newsroom. And yet, while Murray's early years were ones of struggle, his overall life story is one largely of triumph. After becoming the youngest person at the time to win a Pulitzer Prize in 1948, Murray went on to work at *Time* magazine and then on to a successful career as a freelance writer before joining the English Department at UNH at age 39 to teach journalism. At UNH, he quickly transitioned to a new career, advancing through the ranks to become a full professor in 1968. A few years later he served as director of Freshman English and then, briefly, as English Department chair. During his years as a faculty member Murray helped establish a journalism program, a master's degree in teaching, and two doctoral programs in composition and literacy. He was awarded emeritus status upon his retirement in 1987. Beyond campus, in hotel ballrooms, conference halls, and in the pages of the field's journals, Murray helped found a new academic discipline during the final quarter of the twentieth century and penned what would become one of the field's founding documents, "Teach Writing as A Process Not Product." He published fourteen books and textbooks and countless articles and essays about writing and teaching. Murray's life and accomplishments are nothing short of astounding. Having spent years researching him it has been difficult not to conclude that he fit more into a single lifetime than most of us could ever dream of or imagine.

~~~

Of course, Murray was not perfect. He could be rigid and inflexible, was occasionally jealous or petulant, sometimes made bad decisions, and struggled to accept criticism, including from his students, who, as their course evaluations attest, sometimes felt that he failed to understand their need for more guidance and criticism and less support and enthusiasm. "I have never met another person who is more thin-skinned than I am," Murray once wrote of himself, and yet, he was capable of growth and change (*A Writer Teaches Writing,* 2nd ed. 237). The charismatic, larger-than-life World War II veteran and newspaperman who regularly stood before hundreds of teachers to deliver the message that they needed to teach less and listen more spent much of his later life trying to recover from a childhood in which he felt he wasn't listened to at all. Murray was, despite his status as a product of what Neil Lerner has called composition's "star making machine" (217), very, very human—a father, a son, a husband, a colleague, a mentor, and a friend.

More than anything else, though, Murray was an obsessive, driven, ambitious striver of a man. The year of his talk in Iowa City he published an anthology for college students, *Read to Write,* for which he also wrote a 37,000-word instructor's manual. He completed a revised edition of another textbook (i.e., *Write to Learn*). He published five essays in edited collections and placed articles in *College Composition and Communication, Rhetoric Review,* and the *Iowa English Bulletin.* Six of his already-published pieces, aimed at audiences from primary school teachers to college professors, were reprinted that year. In his capacity as a writing consultant/coach, Murray gave workshops for journalists and reporters that year at the Poynter Institute for Media Studies, *The Providence Journal-Bulletin, USA Today,* and *Time.* Within composition and rhetoric, he was elected to the executive committee of the Conference on College Composition and Communication (CCCC) and served as the chair of a committee of the National Council of Teachers of English (NCTE). He gave fifty-two invited talks, lectures, and addresses that year to audiences from Florida to Montreal, New York City to California. He met to discuss writing with executives at CBS Publishing in San Diego, college English professors in Seattle, telephone workers in Boston, journalists and editors in Washington, D.C., junior college instructors in Des Moines, schoolteachers in Pinellas County, Florida, and a freshman English class at an Air Force base near his home in the New Hampshire seacoast. And while it may seem hard to believe, Murray's schedule for 1985 was not unusual or atypical. Virtually every year from the time he published *A Writer Teaches Writing* in 1968 until his retirement in 1987 (and beyond) Murray crisscrossed the country, spreading the good word about process pedagogy and response teaching. As one of his students put it on a course evaluation at UNH,

"The one major problem with [Murray] is that there's only one of him. Everybody wants a piece—myself included—and I don't know how he holds up under the strain. He's like money—the more you get of him, the more you want."

~ ~ ~

Those in composition who are not familiar with Donald Murray or know little about him may see only the stereotype, the kindly, paternal "expressivist" whose ideas about writing and teaching sometimes seem outdated, antiquated—remnants of an earlier and bygone era in the field. As I will show, however, Murray was complex and multifaceted. He was

- a crusader on behalf of education's marginalized—the daydreamers, the misunderstood, the inaccurately labeled, the square pegs who forever fail to fit into education's round holes;
- an innovator whose outsider status in higher education allowed him to imagine and propose solutions to problems in the teaching and researching of writing that others failed to recognize or even understand;
- a collaborator who drew others, and especially those on the disciplinary margins of English, to his side to upend the status quo of the disciplinary applecart;
- a reformer who, despite his writerly accomplishments, deputized as Writer anyone and everyone who approached him to talk about the craft;
- an enemy of snobbery, elitism, arrogance, and privilege, all of which he found in too-great evidence in college English departments (including his own);
- a generous and supportive colleague whose exhaustive service to his institution went far beyond that of the typical college professor; and
- a poet who quietly published on his major themes (i.e., family and childhood, school and war, parenting and old age) throughout his career.

Most importantly and despite what you may have heard, Murray was a pragmatist, unattached to dogma, open to new evidence, arguments, and answers to the two questions that interested him most: what is writing and how should it be taught? "Too often," he writes in a late reconsideration, "I have given the false impression that [when we write] we do one thing, then another, when in fact we do many things simultaneously" ("Response of a Lab Rat" 172). In this instance and in others like it, Murray modeled a scholar who is never fully formed, forever open to new information, always still in the process of becoming.

~~~

Despite attempts to categorize Murray in ways that have caused several generations of writing teachers and scholars to treat him with skepticism, at best, and an attitude of casual dismissal, at worst, Donald Murray has endured.[2] In composition and rhetoric his publications are still cited, although less frequently than they once were. Beyond the immediate borders of our field (and nation) we can find considerable evidence of the persistence of Murray's arguments and ideas in numerous areas of scholarship, including teacher education (Daniels and Beck; Graham; Kerbs; Pasternak et al.), pedagogies and theories of agency and empowerment (Young; Zugnoni), instructional strategies for revision (Coomber), adult learning pedagogies (Wlodkowski & Ginsberg), approaches and methods of conference teaching (Anderson), pedagogies of health/healing (Bird; Bird & Wanner), pedagogies of reflection (Zugnoni), and ESL/EFL instruction (Imelda et al.; Mayes). Many of those who draw on Murray's work today hail from regions far beyond our U.S. borders, with researchers and teachers from Japan (Coomber), Brazil (ÉBida), Indonesia (Imelda et al.), Saudi Arabia (Almutared), and Libya (Al Sabiri & Ersel Kaymakamoğlu) citing Murray's books and articles in their work.

Closer to home, in U.S. composition and rhetoric, Murray's writing still appears in key anthologies and collections used to socialize newcomers to the field (i.e., *Cross Talk*, *The Norton Guide to Composition Studies*) and is still cited by scholars working in various sub-areas including writing technology (Palmeri), history (Peary), and disciplinary identity formation (Combs). Many of Murray's books and textbooks are still in print and with the recent inclusion of various of his essays within curricula aimed at first-year students, his ideas now find currency among a new generation of young writers. A quick google search of certain of his titles included in Doug Downs and Elizabeth Wardle's textbook *Writing about Writing* reveals that college students are reading and writing about Murray a good deal these days, sharing their thoughts about his ideas and arguments in blog posts, on discussion forums, and in Prezi's. In all these ways, Murray lives on. Sixteen years after his death, thirty-plus years after his retirement from teaching, and fifty or more years after he published the "rallying cry" (McLeod 67) that inspired an entire generation of writing teachers and administrators to rethink their approach to composition pedagogy, Donald Murray still speaks to us about writing and its teaching if we are willing to listen.

This book is my attempt to help us do so.

---

2   For readers unfamiliar with Murray's writing or wishing to get a fuller sense of it I suggest Thomas Newkirk and Lisa Miller's excellent edited collection, *The Essential Donald Murray: Lessons from America's Greatest Writing Teacher.*

A WRITER REFORMS (THE TEACHING OF) WRITING: DONALD MURRAY AND THE WRITING PROCESS MOVEMENT, 1963–1987

INTRODUCTION.

WHAT WE TALK ABOUT WHEN WE TALK ABOUT DONALD MURRAY: FROM EXPRESSIVIST TO REFORMER

[H]istorians in rhetoric and composition are more than storytellers who invite listeners to sit at separate fires to learn separate tales of the past. They are also teachers. It is the historian's responsibility to teach us a variety of ways to read the past, to engage in historical debate, to position narratives in relation to each other so as to gain critical perspective, to draw conclusions on and consider implications of opposing historical projects, and to create constructive tension that moves us forward in our inquiry.

– Kathleen A. Welsch, "Review"

Like most brilliant insights, Don's comments on writing were of the "what you didn't know you already really knew" variety. That is, they felt so intuitively and immediately true that you couldn't help but wonder how you had never come to them on your own. I suspect that is one reason why Don's contributions to our field have sometimes been underestimated: many of his insights about the processes of writing and teaching have become so deeply embedded in our practices that we often forget their source.

– Lad Tobin, "Why Murray Matters"

I was several years into this project when Linda Adler-Kassner and Elizabeth Wardle's collection *Naming What We Know: Threshold Concepts of Writing Studies* was published and quickly appeared on my "to read" list (and, just as quickly, on my course syllabi). "[F]ifty (plus) years of research has led us to know some things about the subject of composed knowledge and the questions we ask related to this broad term," Adler-Kassner and Wardle write in the book's Introduction. Their collection, they go on to explain, "represents an effort to bring together those things we know" (59).

As excited as I was about *Naming What We Know*, and as much fun as I had introducing its threshold concepts to students, I initially failed to connect the book with my research into the life and work of Donald M. Murray. Then one day I found myself discussing threshold concept 4.2, Failure Can Be an Important Part of Writing Development, with a group of students and the connection became too obvious to miss. As I walked back to my office after class, my mind kept returning to Murray's *The Craft of Revision*, a book with which I had taught during my first years in the classroom. Pulling my old, dog-eared copy off the shelf I skimmed to the first chapter, "Rewrite Before Writing," and read the two epigraphs Murray includes there:

> Fail. Fail again. Fail Better. (Samuel Beckett)

> I've missed more than 9000 shots in my career. I've lost almost 300 games. 26 times, I've been trusted to take the game win-ning shot and missed. I've failed over and over and over again in my life. And that is why I succeed. (Michael Jordan)

Failure was, I recalled as I read, a big part of Murray's approach to composition pedagogy. At my desk, a quick review of my research blog revealed, further, that failure was something Murray started writing about way back in 1968, in the early days of his career as a college English professor. In "Give Your Students the Writer's Five Experiences" he writes, "Sometimes the first draft may be the final draft, but usually the writer tries to say something, and fails, and through failure tries to say it better, and fails, but perhaps, eventually, he says it well enough" (8). Fast forward almost twenty-five years to 1991, the year of the publication of the first edition of *The Craft of Revision*, and Murray was still writing about failure:

> This book is an invitation. It is not a typical textbook in which the author, an expert on the subject, lectures and instructs, presenting the writer's ideas on history, absolute principles on economics, theories of psychology or law, the laws of physics.

> This book is different because the author is still learning to write. Each page reflects what I am learning as I write and rewrite this textbook. Write along with me. Try your own experiments in meaning, use your language to explore your world as I use my language to explore my world.

> It is all a matter of trial and instructive error. I try to say what I cannot say and fail but find failure instructive. It shows me another way to attempt to say what I have not before said. Fail with me. (5)

Fail with me. It's vintage Murray, speaking the unspeakable with an ironic wink and a smile.

As it turns out, however, and as I soon realized, this passage from *The Craft of Revision* suggests other connections between Murray and what we were now claiming to know about writing. When Murray writes, "This book is different because the author is still learning to write. Each page reflects what I am learning as I write and rewrite this textbook," it's hard not to think of threshold concept 4.0, All Writers Have More to Learn. When Murray urges readers to "Try your own experiments in meaning, use your language to explore your world as I use my language to explore my world" one can hear echoes of threshold concept 1.3, Writing Expresses and Shares Meaning to be Reconstructed by the Reader. When, later in the section I have quoted from above, Murray writes "Try what you can't yet write and as you draft a topic that you think you do not know, you may find that you know more than you thought you did" it is not difficult to summon to mind threshold concept 1.1, Writing is a Knowledge-Making Activity. And when Murray writes, again, later in this section, "[A]s you continue to rewrite, you will find that the subject comes clear," one cannot help but think of threshold concept 4.4, Revision is Central to Developing Writing. In sum, a quick skim of the opening pages of *The Craft of Revision* reveals numerous opportunities to trace what we were now saying we knew about writing to Donald Murray.

Replacing *Craft* on my shelf and picking up *Naming What We Know* I began a search for Murray's name. Coming up empty in the index I searched in the various lists of citations at the end of each of the book's five chapters. When he was nowhere to be found there, either, I quickly reviewed the book's Introduction to try to better understand Adler-Kassner and Wardle's editorial process. In their effort to concisely articulate the field's knowledge, they write, their contributors "set about looking at the research and theory to determine what they could agree we collectively know" (63). Surely Murray, who, between 1963 and 2006 wrote twelve books about writing and its teaching and published fourteen articles in NCTE-sponsored journals alone, was part of the research and theory the contributors examined? If so, readers of *Naming What We Know* wouldn't know it. The book contains not a single reference to or citation of Donald Murray.

Now, in pointing out this omission my intention is not to blame Adler-Kassner and Wardle or the contributors to their collection. Murray's absence in *Naming What We Know*, I am sure, was not intentional. It is his *presence*, at least to those who know how to look for it, that makes his absence in the collection so conspicuous. For if Donald Murray is not credited, less than ten years after his death, in a collection as significant and momentous as *Naming What We Know*, with helping to establish what we now say we know about writing in the field of composition and rhetoric, with what is he credited? Asked differently (and with a nod to Raymond Carver), if not failure, lifelong learning, the social construction of meaning, writing-as-knowledge-making, and the importance of revision, what *do* we talk about when we talk about Donald Murray in the field these days?

DONALD MURRAY = EXPRESSIVIST

For decades two narratives have circulated about Murray within the broad universe of our field. The first, largely a local story forwarded by members of the community of writers, teachers, and researchers who grew up around Murray at UNH in the 1960s, 1970s, and 1980s, is a "Great Man" tale. Within this narrative Murray, author of "Teach Writing as a Process Not Product," an essay that has come to function as a kind of disciplinary "Declaration of Independence" for the field, shines as a heroic figure leading a revolution against the educational and disciplinary establishment. Well-suited to play the part of the "Great Man," Murray, a survivor of the Great Depression and World War II, reached the pinnacle of success in American journalism in the mid 1950s when he won a Pulitzer Prize for editorial writing, became an editor at *Time* magazine and then an accomplished and prolific freelance writer who placed essays and stories in some of the most well-known general interest publications of the post-war era. Transitioning to college teaching in 1963, the very year that many identify as the moment of the modern field's founding (Bridwell-Bowles; Carillo; Connors; Crowley; North; Smit), Murray functions as a kind of George Washington of our field. In penning our disciplinary Declaration of Independence, he may also be our Thomas Jefferson.

The second narrative about Murray circulates in the wider field of composition and rhetoric and positions him quite differently. If Murray plays the Great Man in the first account he functions as a figure of embarrassment, even ridicule, in the second due to his association with expressionistic rhetoric or expressivism. As an expressivist, Murray was deemed an advocate of a politically naïve and ineffectual writing pedagogy that failed to account for the socio-cultural and political aspects of composing. No one has narrated the story about how Murray (and Elbow and Macrorie) was marginalized in the late 1980s and 1990s more memorably than Wendy Bishop, who writes:

> Elbow and Murray were made safe by transformation into
> figures, by relegation to expressivist categories. Then, as the
> field professionalized, there followed a progression of dimin-
> ishment and tuckings-away, a little like the nouveau riche
> habit of sticking the money-earning but foolishly-dressed
> grandfather in the back study, not introducing him to high
> society company where he might embarrass. (24)

Here, Bishop provides us with a striking image to grasp the second narrative about Murray: the "foolishly-dressed grandfather" or, in Murray's case, the foolish expressivist who still asks students to pen personal essays and read tired expository pieces by writers like E.B. White. If Murray plays the part of the hero in the first story, in the second he's more the fool.

Of these two narratives, the latter, I would argue, has had the greater purchase and staying power, giving birth to a conceptual frame, *Donald Murray = Expressivist*, that has, despite the efforts of those who have sought to resist or negate it (see Ballenger; Newkirk, "Donald Murray and the 'Other Self'"; Tobin; Williams), been highly influential in shaping our disciplinary understanding and conception of Murray. It's become what we talk about when we talk about Donald Murray. The linguist George Lakoff defines conceptual frames, and *Donald Murray = Expressivist* is surely a good example of one, as "mental structures that shape the way we see the world" (xv). All words, Lakoff argues, are understood within and "defined relative to conceptual frames." Words "activate" frames in our brains and once these are established they're difficult to shake. "Thinking differently," Lakoff asserts, "requires speaking differently" and speaking differently—about Murray, about anyone—as teachers of rhetoric know all too well, is no simple task.

I have lived uncomfortably with what the historian Lynée Lewis Gaillet calls the "traditional 'truth'" of the *Donald Murray = Expressivist* frame since I first encountered it while reading James Berlin's (in)famous article "Rhetoric and Ideology in the Writing Class" in a graduate seminar in the early 2000s. I am not the first to be troubled by it but, as Bronwyn Williams acknowledges, there are limits to what one can accomplish when attempting to refute a dominant and established frame. "Like so many of my 'expressivist' friends" Williams writes of his efforts to push back against *Donald Murray = Expressivist*,

> I feel as if I am fighting on someone else's terms to have some-one like Don Murray taken seriously again. . . . It is a defensive position, marked by attempts to re-label ourselves, qualify our statements, maintain that we are not "merely or simply expressivist" (22) and, yes, argue that Don Murray's work is based on theoretical assumptions that have not been adequately recognized. For our efforts we get lightly dismissed, like bright young children who don't yet understand how the world really works.

According to linguist Lakoff, "how the world really works" is that the best way *not* to change a conceptual frame is to attempt to refute it (hence the title of Lakoff's popular book, *Don't Think of an Elephant*). To really change a frame, Lakoff argues, a communicator must reclaim "the power to decide what's important" by creating a new frame "to reset the terms of discussion or debate" (xv). And therein lies my purpose in this book. In attempting to reframe Murray, my argument is simple: Donald Murray should be understood and remembered *not* as a proponent of a single approach to composition pedagogy but, rather, as a *reformer* of an academic discipline, English, that he felt shortchanged writing and its teaching and an educational system that he felt all too often disenfranchised students.

I draw this term, *reformer*, from the work of the late Robert Connors, Murray's colleague at UNH. In his wide-ranging *Composition-Rhetoric: Backgrounds, Theory, and Pedagogy*, Connors posits that in the 1960s, during the years Murray was transitioning from journalist/freelancer to college English professor, three new groups of scholars, researchers, and theorists emerged to challenge the dominant paradigm in composition (i.e., current-traditional rhetoric). For students of Berlin, two of Connors' three groups, the New Rhetoricians (later, social-constructivists) and the Empiricists (or cognitivists), likely sound familiar. Connors' coins a different term, however, to describe his third group: the Reformers (or writing process theorists). These teacher-scholars, Connors argues, were "concerned not so much with what students were taught as how they were taught." He continues:

> In the minds of these teachers, the problem with composi-
> tion-rhetoric went deeper than mere issues of content, and
> the received methods of teaching writing were not merely
> inefficient or unworkable. The way in which composition was
> taught, to these theorists, was at best a bad method. At worst,
> it was actively destructive, leading to desiccation of the stu-
> dent's creativity, to useless fear about meaningless (and proba-
> bly fictional) entities such as Emphasis and The Paragraph or
> Comparison and Contrast, to writer's block, paranoia about
> mechanical issues, and to dead, imitative, ponderous student
> prose that attempted to mimic the dead, imitative, ponderous
> prose of academia. (16)

In Connors' articulation of the Reformers, I find a vivid and accurate depiction of the Donald Murray I have come to know over the course of the dozen or so years I have spent investigating his life and work. In borrowing and forwarding this frame, *reformer*, I seek, per Lakoff, to "reset the terms of discussion or debate" about Murray. By historicizing him, which is to say by placing him, per Gaillet, "within the framework and exigence of [his] times," I seek to reframe Murray for a new generation of composition teachers and scholars and establish a new legacy for him rooted in the historical details of his accomplishments in and contributions to our field (36).

REFRAMING DONALD MURRAY

Reframing Murray, as I attempt to do in this book, can profitably begin with an examination of the roots of the conceptual frame that has so come to define him.

Donald Murray = Expressivist was borne out of efforts in the 1970s and 1980s to describe the theories, philosophies, and rhetorics guiding composition pedagogy at the time (see Berlin, "Contemporary Composition," "Rhetoric and Ideology"; Faigley; Fulkerson, "Composition Theory in the Eighties," "Four Philosophies of Composition"; Lynn). Of those conducting such inquiries, some chose to point to specific theorists as exemplars of particular approaches while others left it up to readers to determine which theorists might be slotted into which camps—or even whether slotting was, in the first place, a wise endeavor. Of the taxonomizers only Berlin explicitly links Murray with expressivism, doing so for the first time in *Rhetoric and Reality*, where he asserts that Murray should be understood as "one of the leading expressionists of the sixties and seventies" (151) and, for the second time, in "Rhetoric and Ideology," where he mounts a full-throated critique of and attack on expressionistic rhetoric and on those he identifies as its chief advocates (Murray, but also Elbow and Macrorie). For those unfamiliar with or simply long past Berlin's arguments, I'd like to linger on them a moment, especially those presented in "Rhetoric and Ideology," since they have had such influence in the field for so long.[1]

"Rhetoric and Ideology" builds on and extends Berlin's earlier article, "Contemporary Composition: The Major Pedagogical Theories" in which he describes the four pedagogical approaches he finds most evident in the teaching of composition and rhetoric at the time (i.e., Neo-Aristotelian or Classicist, Positivist or Current-Traditionalist, Neo-Platonist or Expressionist, and New Rhetorical), and argues, however lightly, for the New Rhetorical approach. If anyone plays the villain in "Contemporary Composition" it's the Positivists or Current-Traditionalists, who, by 1982, most in our field agreed were largely responsible for the decades-old failures of composition pedagogy. "Neo-Platonic, Neo-Aristotelian, and what I have called New Rhetoric," Berlin explains in "Contemporary Composition," are "reactions to the inadequacy of Current-Traditional Rhetoric to teach students a notion of the composing process that will enable them to become effective persons as they become effective writers" (777). While Berlin admits that his own "sympathies" are with the New Rhetoric, he argues that the three approaches "can be considered as one in their efforts to establish new directions for a modern rhetoric" (777). Notably, in his articulation of the Neo-Platonist or Expressionist approach, Berlin references neither Murray nor Elbow. Significantly, the polemical in "Contemporary Composition" is largely subverted to the expository. Berlin's purpose seems less to argue than to describe.

---

1   This may be because "Rhetoric and Ideology" was long anthologized in one of the field's most popular collections used in graduate education, *Cross-Talk in Comp Theory: A Reader*. Notably, it was dropped from the book's third and most recent edition.

Fast forward six years, to the publication of "Rhetoric and Ideology," and Berlin's aims had evolved. Whereas in "Contemporary Composition" he was largely interested in describing approaches to composition pedagogy, in "Rhetoric and Ideology" he moves on from describing to critiquing the classroom rhetorics he finds most problematic and arguing for the rhetoric he deems most well-suited to a new goal, seemingly unrelated to teaching: exposing the "mystifications" of capitalist society.[2] The three rhetorics Berlin discusses in "Rhetoric and Ideology" are, famously, cognitive psychology, expressionism, and social-epistemic rhetoric, with the last being Berlin's preference in that it "places the question of ideology at the center of teaching writing." (Cognitive psychology, in its efforts to discover "objective truth," largely ignores or attempts to circumvent ideology. Expressionist rhetoric, while grounded in a critique of "the ideology of corporate capitalism," (492) is too easily co-opted by the forces it seeks to oppose.) The primary fodder for Berlin's critique of expressionistic rhetoric in "Rhetoric and Ideology" comes from the work of Donald Murray and Elbow, with Berlin drawing on Murray's first book, *A Writer Teaches Writing* and one of his first articles "Finding Your Own Voice in an Age of Dissent" as key sources for his analysis and critique.[3] A careful rereading of "Rhetoric and Ideology" suggests that Berlin's condemnation of expressionistic rhetoric ultimately boils down to its too-great focus on the individual as the locus of social change. "For expressionistic rhetoric," he writes, "the correct response to the imposition of current economic, political, and social arrangements is thus resistance, but a resistance that is always construed in individual terms" (487). Expressionistic rhetoric, he continues, is "inherently and debilitatingly divisive of political protest, suggesting that effective resistance can only be offered by individuals, each acting alone" (487). Contrast this with Berlin's preferred social-epistemic rhetoric, in which "Self-autonomy and self-fulfillment are possible not through becoming detached from the social, but through resisting those social influences that alienate and disempower, [and] doing so, moreover, in and through social activity" (491). If expressionists like Murray and Elbow and social-epistemics like Berlin share common ground, it seems, it is in their concern about the problem of alienation that individuals experience because of "the material conditions of [their] existence," (490). Where they seem to differ, however, is in their remedy (i.e., Murray/Elbow = individual empowerment; Berlin = social protest).

---

2   Why or how does this matter to what writing teachers do in the classroom, one might ask. "[A] way of teaching is never innocent," Berlin warns his readers near the end "Rhetoric and Ideology." "Every pedagogy is imbricated in ideology" (492).

3   It's amazing to discover, given the impact and longevity of Berlin's arguments, that in "Rhetoric and Ideology" he draws on just two of Murray's publications as evidence for his assertions, each of which was almost a quarter century old at the time he was writing.

DONALD MURRAY = EXPRESSIVIST . . . ?

As scholars David Gold and David Stock have pointed out, Berlin's taxonomies have had substantial impact on our field's understanding of its disciplinary past. As Gold puts it, "Rhetoric and composition historiography might be considered a series of footnotes to Berlin" (19–20). For Stock, Berlin "has had an enduring and disproportionate influence on Writing Studies' perception of its history and pedagogies," his histories and taxonomies "often treated as historical facts rather than as social constructions" (193). As Maureen Daly Goggin reminds us, "History, like any scholarly endeavor, is after all a rhetorical act" (xv). While we cannot, of course, blame Berlin entirely for the marginalization that led to the establishment of the conceptual frame *Donald Murray = Expressivist*, we can investigate the ways in which the frame he helped create has been taken up and re-inscribed, largely without question or qualification, by subsequent scholars and historians of the discipline. In what follows, I examine one such instance, to better understand the way the frame has been activated and to investigate whether it stands up in the face of a more nuanced reading of Murray's work.

In a chapter of their book *1977: A Cultural Moment in Composition* which examines the "national conversation" about composition teaching in the late 1970s via a case study focused on Penn State University, Brent Henze, Jack Selzer, and Wendy Sharer examine two "student-centered pedagogies," expressivism and cognitivism, which, they argue, following Berlin, first emerged as critiques of and responses to the dominant teaching approaches of the day (i.e., New Criticism and current-traditional rhetoric). Expressivism and cognitivism, Henze et al. assert, share a good deal in common, including their conception of "the relative autonomy of writers from social circumstances," and yet they compete for priority in the field as they promote "different basic principles and pedagogical strategies" (31). First, expressivists, and here Henze et al. identify the usual suspects, i.e., Macrorie, Elbow, Murray, hold that "formal instruction [in writing] [i]s more or less incidental to a writer's growth" (33). Second, within expressivist pedagogies, they argue, students are to be "regarded as independent agents—even teachers and textbooks [a]re irrelevant—who c[an] intuit principles of effective writing through trial and error" (33). And third, unlike advocates of the cognitivist school, whose central concern is teaching "communicative effectiveness," proponents of expressivism emphasize "personal growth, authenticity, self-discovery, and voice" (32–33). In sum, as Henze et al. define it, a writing course for expressivists is largely "a matter of a teacher's nurturing student self-discovery and self-expression" (33).

As we see, Henze et al. are working in the shadow of Berlin, adapting, or adopting his categories, defining terms in ways that are similar to and mostly

11

aligned with his. My question, simply, is does it hold up? Does it work? Are there basic "principles and pedagogical strategies" that we can say apply to all (or even most) of those who have been identified with expressivism, or, minimally, in this case, to Donald Murray? "All of these [expressivist] values were already guiding the pedagogy of Donald Murray," Henze et al. assert as they go on to cite two of his mid-career publications (i.e., "Write Before Writing" and "Writing as Process: How Writing Finds Its Own Meaning"), as evidence for their claim that Murray "nurture[d] expressivism into the 1980s" (33).[4] Clearly, for Henze et al., there is little doubt that the terms and categories Berlin bequeathed to us are real, coherent, and largely accurate. There is no need for qualification. The *Donald Murray = Expressivist* frame can be (and is) invoked without much thought or critical consideration.

But was Donald Murray concerned with students' personal growth? Did he advocate for writerly authenticity? Was he an advocate of self-discovery through writing? And was voice a central matter of his concern?

The answers to these questions are, at various points in Murray's career, yes, yes, yes, and yes. And yet, things are not so simple.

Let's take Henze et al.'s first point, that for expressivists "formal instruction [i]s more or less incidental to a writer's growth." It is difficult to align this way of thinking with Donald Murray, at any stage of his career. Murray's argument, from the moment he entered the field, was that the kind of formal writing instruction typical in schools, provided by teachers who did not write and were usually trained to teach literature, was not just incidental to but actually *detrimental to* students' writerly growth. The solution, however, was not the elimination of formal instruction. Rather, it was formal instruction of *a different* sort. Murray's first book about writing, *A Writer Teaches Writing: A Practical Method of Teaching Composition*, directed at an audience of those delivering formal instruction in writing, i.e., high school English teachers, provides a glimpse into his initial vision of what alternate formal instruction in writing might look like. No, Murray did not want to eliminate formal writing instruction in schools, and he did not want to get rid of writing teachers. Teachers were, in fact, the *very people* he most wanted to reach, so that he could offer them new and different ways to instruct.

There is a second crucial point to make about Henze et al.'s invocation of the *Donald Murray = Expressivist* frame in *1977*. As "independent agents," they write, students were to "intuit principles of effective writing through trial and error." As

---

4   That Henze et al. cite "Writing as Process" to bolster their claims is an indication of the power of confirmation bias, for this article stands out above almost all of Murray's other publications as the least "expressivist" in nature and as the clearest example of the extent to which Murray was, by 1980, working to adopt his writing to the new social science paradigm within the field. I will discuss this in greater detail in Chapter 4.

we have seen, Murray never conceived of students as "independent agents" and while it is true to say that he wanted students to learn to write through a process resembling trial and error, it's not true to say that he wanted them to "intuit" a set of principles of effective writing because he did not believe such things existed. When Murray first came to UNH in 1963 writing had been taught, at least in freshman English, via a top-down, deductive process whereby students were first taught abstract, conceptual knowledge about writing (i.e., unity, coherence, emphasis, etc.) and then asked to apply and demonstrate their knowledge of these concepts via written themes. Murray objected to this approach and argued for a more inductive method, whereby students would write first and then reflect— but *not* on a set of principles of effective writing. Rather, Murray wanted them to reflect on what they were learning about the process of writing by practicing it. It was not so much *principles* Murray was after as it was *process*, for as we learn elsewhere in his work Murray's approach to principles was less prescriptive than it was rhetorical. "I think there are many good and right ways to write, depending on the content, the writer and the audience," he explains in a newspaper article he published circa 1976 ("City Boy Finds Woods" A31). A few years earlier he had made this same point in his first published article in *College English*: "There is no right and wrong in writing. There is what works and what doesn't work" ("Perhaps the Professor" 170). Finally, Murray surely didn't believe teachers and textbooks to be irrelevant. His approach to composition pedagogy was, ultimately, centered around the student-teacher conference. Teachers, properly trained, were essential to the process. As to textbooks, as someone who penned an entire curriculum series aimed at grade school children (i.e., *Write to Communicate: The Language Arts in Process*) and several textbooks aimed at college students (i.e., *Write to Learn* and *Read to Write*), Murray surely did not think such work irrelevant.

A final point: in the third passage cited above, Henze et al. invoke the now well-established point about the importance to expressivist pedagogies of writing-for-self-discovery. They call on the work of Donald Stewart to help make this argument:

> The primary goal of any writing course is self-discovery
> for the student and . . . the most visible indication of that
> self-discovery is the appearance, in the student's writing, of an
> authentic voice. (qtd. in Henze et al. 32)

At the start of his career, in the middle, and at the end, Donald Murray would not have agreed with the statement "the primary goal of any writing course is self-discovery for the student." Self-discovery, in the sense of writing-as-a-means-to-better-self-understanding (which is how I read Stewart's words), was not a primary goal of a composition course for Murray, although late in his life, as he, himself, sought to come to terms with the emotionally challenging aspects of his childhood, Murray came to appreciate and even advocate for the cathartic or therapeutic potentialities of writing (and was among the earliest in our field to do so). But "writing as therapy," as some have called it, was never Murray's primary or even secondary goal.

Rather, his objective, throughout his career, was to help students become more engaged, thoughtful, reflective and, therefore, effective communicators. To do so he shared with them the experiential knowledge he had gained as a professional writer as well as the new knowledge he was gaining, in the 1970s and 1980s, as a deep reader in the emergent composing process research of the field. As they contrast expressivists with cognitivists, Henze et al. argue that what separated the two was a primary concern, on the part of expressivists, with "self discovery" and on the part of cognitivists with "communicative effectiveness." If these are the options and if we must continue to categorize our theorists, I believe that Murray might more accurately be placed among the cognitivists, for he was more concerned with teaching students to communicate effectively than he was with teaching them to write for self-discovery (a both/and synthesis, were such an option possible, might, however, be the most fitting for Murray). If not out of a concern for communicative effectiveness, why else would Murray have spent so much of his career (all of it, in fact) trying to map out the various stages or phases of the writing process, so as to identify a transferable model of writing that could be taught to students in order that they could communicate effectively regardless of the rhetorical situation?

There's another important point to be made here about the *Donald Murray = Expressivist* frame as it is invoked by Henze et al., however, and one not to be missed: Donald Murray was a non-traditional scholar, to be sure, but perhaps not atypical of his era in the sense that many (most?) of his publications lack textual citations or references to the work of other researchers.[5] When Murray did cite others, however, beginning around the mid to late 1970s, he rarely called on the work of those with whom he is typically associated—so-called expressivists like Stewart, Macrorie, or Elbow. No, Murray's citations were almost always of so-called cognitivists, folks like Sondra Perl, Janet Emig, Donald Graves, Linda Flower, Carol Chomsky, and others who were mobilizing social science methodologies to try to find answers to the very questions about writing that Murray had been asking for years. Further, as early as 1970 Murray had begun to issue calls for writing research of the very sort scholars like Perl or Graves would

---

5   Note that I've used the word "researchers" here. Throughout his career, Murray was prolific in referencing the words of writers—novelists, poets, journalists—to bolster his claims, to the point where he eventually published a book, *Shoptalk: Learning to Write with Writers*, to collect the hundreds of quotes about writing that he had amassed over the years.

eventually take up (sadly, none, aside from Graves, ever cited him as providing the exigence for their inquiries). "More scholars," Murray writes in "The Interior View," "using information from the social sciences and the sciences should be encouraged to contribute to the study of the writing process" (21). No surprise, then, that when such research began to appear in the pages of our field's major journals, Murray took notice and began to incorporate it into his work. Here are several examples from one of the articles Henze et al. reference, "Writing as Process: How Writing Finds its Own Meaning," a piece that comes as close to a social science research report as Murray was capable of writing:

> Others of us, instructed by Janet Emig (1975), attempt to understand the relationship between the chemical and electrical interaction within the brain . . . (Newkirk and Miller 6)

> The term rehearsing, first used by my colleague Donald Graves (1978) after observation of children writing . . . (Newkirk and Miller 8)

> As Perl (1979) has documented, we write and react to those marks on paper . . . (Newkirk and Miller 14)

These passages are just several examples drawn from one article in which Murray works to position himself within the emergent conversation about writing that so-called "cognitivist" writing researchers like Emig, Graves, and Perl were initiating in the mid 1970s. There are others. Especially after Graves joined the UNH faculty in 1974, Murray increasingly worked to conceptualize his ideas and communicate them within a kind of quasi-social science framework and register, and yet these efforts have never, to the best of my knowledge, been acknowledged or examined. Such an analysis surely complicates the *Donald Murray = Expressivist* frame that scholars like Henze et al., following Berlin, invoke all too easily. In sum, established frames must be tested by new generations of scholars. If they are found wanting, as I am suggesting is the case with *Donald Murray = Expressivist*, new frames must be created.

RISE AND FALL OF A REFORMER

While Berlin's histories have, as Gold and Stock have argued, been highly influential in shaping our collective understanding of our disciplinary past, the irony, at least in the case of Donald Murray, is that in the years leading up to the publication of Berlin's key works in the 1980s, Murray had, by any number of measures, come to stand near or at center-stage in composition and rhetoric. By the mid 1980s Murray was placing articles and essays in the leading journals of the day, including those aimed at K–12 English and language arts teachers, college English professors, journalism educators, and more general educational readers.[6] His status in the field of K–12 language arts education was so well-established that he was invited by the editors of *Language Arts* and *The English Journal* to contribute assessments on the current and future state of the field. Further, Murray's work was widely reprinted at this time. In 1986. his article "The Maker's Eye: Revising Your Own Manuscripts" was reprinted six times (Murray, "Faculty Annual Report, 1985–86"). Finally, Murray was distinctly present in the pages of NCTE's flagship journal for college-level writing instructors and scholars, *College Composition and Communication* (CCC) during these years. At least two of the articles he placed in *CCC* in the first half of the eighties were lead pieces (i.e., "Teaching the Other Self: The Writer's First Reader" and "One Writer's Secrets"). According to a citation analysis conducted of the journal by Phillips, Greenberg, and Gibson, Murray was the seventh most frequently cited author in *CCC* during the period 1980–1993, ahead of Nancy Sommers, Emig, and Mike Rose.

The range and diversity of Murray's writing at this time is similarly impressive. His published book chapters serve as one illustration of the various purposes for which and audiences to whom he wrote, with chapters appearing in collections on creative writing, rhetoric, professional writing, the discipline of English, composition theory and pedagogy, and in books aimed at mainstream audiences seeking writing advice.[7] As Moran points out, Murray's ideas in these essays, as well as in his published journal articles, were taken up and used by scholars theorizing diverse areas in the field, including writing center theory, one-on-one conference teaching, and computers and writing (136). In the area of textbooks, Murray was also productive during the 1980s, penning three new titles[8] and, in

---

6   The pieces aimed at K–12 English and language arts teachers were published in *The English Journal, Language Arts*, and *English Education*; the essays directed at an audience of college English professors appeared in *College English, College Composition and Communication, The Journal of Basic Writing, Freshman English News, Rhetoric Review*; the piece aimed at journalism educators was published in the journal *Style*; and the article aimed at a general educational audience appeared in *The Journal of Education*.

7   Murray's essay on creative writing appeared in *Creative Writing in America* (Moxley); his work on rhetoric was published in *Sentence Combining: A Rhetorical Perspective* (Daiker) and *Reinventing the Rhetorical Tradition* (Freedman & Pringle); his essays on professional writing appeared in *Worlds of Writing: Teaching and Learning in Discourse Communities of Work* (Matalene), and *Writing for Many Roles* (Schwartz); his essay on English was published in *Education in the Eighties: English* (Shuman); his articles on composition theory and pedagogy appeared in *Eight Approaches to Teaching Composition* (Donovan & McClelland), *When a Writer Can't Write: Studies in Writer's Block and Other Composing-Process Problems* (Rose), and *Only Connect: Uniting Reading and Writing* (Newkirk); and his writing on writing for mainstream audiences appeared in *Writers on Writing* (Waldrep).

8   *Writing for Your Readers*, a practical book on writing for journalists; *Write to Learn* and *Read to Write*, textbooks aimed at college audience.

1985, an entirely revised edition of *A Writer Teaches Writing*. Reviews of these books highlight Murray's significance and stature among his peers at this time. Richard Gephardt, for example, calls Murray "one of America's most respected teachers of writing" (432). Carol Berkenkotter describes him as "a significant tradition in composition studies," (111) and "a major force in American writing pedagogy" (115). John Clifford asserts that "Murray's process-oriented ideas are so woven into our thinking that we forgot who said them first" (99). And Susan McLeod reminds readers that Murray was "one of the earliest to discuss writing as a process and to speculate about how that process could best be taught" (417). The words of these scholars, Murray's contemporaries, further signal the esteem with which he was held by many in the field at this time.

Murray's speaking schedule for any year in the 1980s provides additional evidence of his stature in the eighties. During the 1981–82 academic year, for example, he gave talks, sat on panels, or lead workshops or seminars away from campus over 30 times. In late August, he taught a week-long program for journalists and editors in Raleigh, North Carolina. In early September, he gave a workshop for secondary school teachers in Connecticut. In October, he was a panelist at the international meeting of the Associated Press in Toronto. In November, he gave a lunchtime address at the Conference of English Education at NCTE. In December, he was in Virginia. In January and February, he was in Maine and Rhode Island. In March, he was in Ohio and Texas (Murray, "Faculty Annual Report, 1981–82"). In sum, Murray's yearly travel schedule offers yet another window onto his influence as he approached the final years of his career. It was by no means inevitable, then, that he would become locked in the disabling and debilitating *Donald Murray = Expressivist* frame at this time.

A close look at changes taking place in composition and rhetoric during the late eighties and into the early nineties, however, suggests the seeds of Murray's displacement were, with or without Berlin, being sown at this time. In a 1985 review of Murray's textbook *Write to Learn*, Berkenkotter, with whom Murray had collaborated on an extensive research study just a few years earlier, was among the first to publicly question the efficacy of "the principles Murray represents" (115). In light of shifts in the field that increasingly understood composition pedagogy as serving the ends of academic enculturation, Berkenkotter asserts that "The issue of a student's socialization into the academic disciplines is one that writing teachers must confront if they want their students to succeed in college" (114). It was an issue Murray had dealt with in only a cursory way in *Write to Learn* because it was an issue in which he was, in 1985, but also in 1975, and 1965, largely uninterested in confronting.[9] Murray had an expansive vision

---

9   In a late-life interview, Murray suggests his understanding of the challenge of devising

of composition pedagogy and never imagined that he was preparing students to write only for academic audiences. "We are teaching writers," he explains in the first edition of *A Writer Teaches Writing*, "boys and girls who will write descriptions of automobile accidents and living room suites which are on sale, reports on factory production and laboratory experiments, political speeches and the minutes of League of Women Voters meetings, love letters and business letters" (154). Here, we see that from the start, Murray's objective was to prepare students for writerly success *wherever* they wrote.

The movement towards teaching writing in the service of academic socialization was, of course, an important element of a larger transition, the so-called "social turn" in composition and rhetoric in the mid to late 1980s and 1990s. Richard Fulkerson, self-nominated chronicler of the field's evolutions (and revolutions) from the late seventies to the early 2000s, captures the changes afoot at this time when he argues that there was a kind of disciplinary consensus forming at this time around a "rhetorical axiology," i.e., pedagogies in which "readers and their responses are the final criteria of [writing's] effectiveness" (415). If, as Fulkerson points out, "genuine and extensive conflicts existed" at this time "about what constituted good writing and thus about what sort of writing one ought to teach," scholars and teachers of composition and rhetoric were, by the late 1980s and early 1990s, aligning behind a socio-rhetorical orientation to composition pedagogy which, as Newkirk, invoking Kenneth Burke, has put it, shifted the field's attention from the "writer" to the "scene of writing" ("Donald Murray and The 'Other Self'" 47). Murray, whose interest in how writing is made and, by extension, how it ought to be taught had always foregrounded the writer and not the reader (or audience) in his investigations. As such, he struggled (or refused?) to adapt or re-align his thinking to attend to the more social and rhetorical aspects of composing which came to dominate the field's discussions of composition pedagogy in the late 1980s and 1990s. Adapt Murray did, though, if only incrementally. "There is no one, correct, theologically sound writing process," he writes in the *Instructor's Manual* for his book *Write to Learn*, circa 1987. Rather, as he explains, the process changes due to several factors—"the cognitive style of the writer; the experience of the writer with a particular task; the psychological makeup of the writer and the psychological climate in which the writing is done; the content of the writing, its purpose, its audience; the length of time in

---

effective discipline-specific pedagogy for first-year writing courses: "When I first taught freshman English, my idea of teaching it was very clear. I thought I'd ask the history students to write history and the psychology students to write psychology and the physicists to write physics. Except I forgot what it was like in school. The psychology majors hadn't yet taken a course in psychology and the historians hadn't studied history, so they had no material yet to write about in those subjects" (Boe, "From the Editor!" 5–6).

which the writer has to work; and the tools the writer is using" (24). Here, we see Murray's continued emphasis on "the writer," but also his accounting for other factors that influence writing, including traditional rhetorical concerns.

To the list of factors that coalesced to shift Donald Murray out of composition and rhetoric's spotlight in the late eighties and early nineties we should add changing publication norms. As Daly Goggin has shown, by 1990 or so journals in composition and rhetoric had become "formal, scholarly forums designed both to accommodate and encourage sophisticated research and scholarship" (139). Murray, of course, had entered the field at a time when the range of what was deemed acceptable in its leading journals was more flexible and when his unique style of essayistic self-inquiry was not just welcomed by journal editors but embraced (and imitated by other writers). It was a time, further, when Murray's chief credential, a Pulitzer Prize, bestowed upon him a kind of credibility that may have come to mean less as the first generation of composition scholars with Ph.D.s assumed control of the field's knowledge-dissemination apparati.[10] Late into his career and without the capacity to conduct "sophisticated research and scholarship," Murray was increasingly left behind by changes in the field's publication norms, a fact which, as we will see, can be measured both anecdotally and quantitatively.

In 1986, Murray published his essay "One Writer's Secrets" in *CCC* where it was positioned as the May issue's lead article. According to Richard Larson's "Editor's Note," "most of the items in the May issue are concerned, broadly speaking, with matters of 'scholarship' and 'research'" (145). Thus, in 1986, Murray's "brand" was considered worthy of kicking off a special issue in the field's flagship journal devoted to matters of scholarship. A few years later Murray submitted another essay to *CCC* for another special issue, this one focused on "Teaching and Theory in College Composition." The piece, "All Writing is Autobiography," was ultimately accepted and published, but not within the special issue area of the volume. Rather, it was placed in the "Staffroom Interchanges" section where, according to the editor's note, "descriptions of specific instructional or administrative practices and fuller essays of application, speculation, and introspection" (66) were discussed.[11] This anecdote signals the rapid decline in the value of Murray's brand over the course of just a few years, at least as measured by his experience with one journal.

---

10   The irony here, that it was folks like Murray who worked to establish the doctoral programs in which the first Ph.D.s who replaced them were trained, should not be missed.

11   Worth noting, further, is the fact that the "Staffroom Interchange" section of the journal had existed in *CCC* at least since Murray published his first article in the journal in the spring of 1969. His earlier work had never been placed there, however. In fact, of the six articles Murray published in *CCC* over the course of his career, three appeared as lead articles.

Further support for the claim that Murray's star was falling in the field by the early 1990s comes from a second *CCC* citation analysis, this one conducted by Derek Mueller on the years 1987–2011. In terms of total citations in the journal during this period, Murray slipped from number seven to number thirty-one. Of the 19,477 citations Mueller examined, Murray was referenced just 46 times, six fewer in the 24-year period of Mueller's analysis than in the 13-year period of Burns Phillips et al.'s (i.e., 1980–1993). These numbers, drawn from the field's flagship journal, signal Murray's decline in visibility and stature within the field during the closing years of the twentieth century and the opening ones of the twenty-first.

And yet, throughout the 1990s and right up until the time of his death in late 2006, Murray continued to play an active role in discussions of writing and pedagogy, albeit outside the bright spotlight of composition and rhetoric's center stage. When he wasn't writing his weekly column on aging for *The Boston Globe*, which began in 1986, or writing his memoirs, Murray continued to write and publish about writing and pedagogy during these years, placing essays and articles in small-scale journals aimed at aspiring writers and/or classroom teachers or edited collections assembled by friends in the UNH community. During this time Murray also wrote and rewrote his textbooks, revising all of his previous books and penning five new titles including two on journalism and two on composition.[12] And he continued to evangelize, giving talks and lectures on writing and writing pedagogy to just about everyone and anyone who was willing to listen.

In sum, in his retirement and on the margins of composition and rhetoric, proper, Donald Murray continued to exert influence on the teaching and study of writing, particularly within New England and particularly among school teachers and writers. His voice may have gone quiet in the field's primary publication venues but Murray was far from silent on the topic of writing and its teaching during the twenty-year period following his retirement from UNH and leading up to his death.

RESEARCHER STANCE AND METHODOLOGY

Robert Connors famously described archival research as "a kind of directed ramble, something like an August mushroom hunt" ("Dreams and Play" 23). My decade-long journey through this project has been a long and fairly *undirected* ramble, with a fortuitous discovery of a substantial trove of shrooms late

---

12   The books on journalism were *Writer in the Newsroom: The Poynter Papers* and *Writing to Deadline: The Journalist at Work*; the books on composition were *The Craft of Revision* and *Crafting a Life in Essay, Story, Poem.*

in the hunt. What, readers may be wondering, has sustained me on this journey and kept me in the forest?

My sustenance has been both personal and professional, and therein, perhaps, lies the cause of its longevity. In *Beyond the Archives: Research as a Lived Experience,* Gesa E. Kirsch and Liz Rohan suggest that "the most serious, committed, excellent historical research comes from choosing a subject to which we are personally drawn." A personal connection, they continue, "brings the subject to life and makes us more likely to pursue hunches, follow leads, and spend extra time combing through archival materials than we would without a 'personal attachment'" (8). So, it is with me. Twice a graduate of UNH and its English department (B.A. 1996; Ph.D. 2007), I came of age as a writer, teacher, and researcher in the years just after Donald Murray's retirement. I met Murray for the first time in the summer of 1996 as I wrapped up my undergraduate coursework and prepared to depart for the University of Iowa, where I pursued a Master of Arts in Teaching (MAT) to become a high school English teacher. At Iowa, I read Murray for the first time in Dr. Bonnie Sunstein's graduate course, Approaches to Teaching Writing (Sunstein, herself, a daughter of UNH) and got to know him a good deal better during my first year as I transcribed dozens of hours of audio interviews he had given Sunstein for a 1997 NCTE session celebrating his career.

Back in New Hampshire in the early 2000s, I enrolled in the doctoral program at UNH and reconnected with Murray to interview him for a graduate paper I was writing on the history of writing conferences. At the same time, as a teaching assistant in my own early classrooms, I experimented with Murray's pedagogical methods, trying out with my students approaches to the teaching of writing which I had experienced at UNH as a student myself just a few years earlier and was now studying in the graduate classroom. Throughout my years in the doctoral program I attended potlucks at Murray's home, at which he held court, regaling students and faculty alike with stories of his life and work and walking us through his latest writerly discoveries. And when Murray passed away in late 2006 I joined the hundreds of mourners who came together to celebrate his life in the Johnson Theater at UNH, just a short walk from Murkland Hall where, sixty years earlier, Murray, himself a UNH alum, had taken his first undergraduate English classes and, twenty years later, taught his first college courses. In sum, "a personal connection to one's research" *has* "ma[d]e all the difference" with this project and it is this connection that has kept me at it these many years. As such, it perhaps goes without saying that this history is far from disinterested. My personal knowledge of my subject and affiliation with the larger community of UNH writers, teachers, and scholars has shaped my inquiry every step of the way.

As to methodology, I can say that since 2009, when I took my first steps in the direction of this project, my research has proceeded through several distinct stages or phases. During Phase I (2009–2011), after being denied a visit to the Poynter Institute for Media Studies where Murray's archive was then housed,[13] I was fortunate to gain partial access to his materials via a librarian, David Shedden, who listened patiently to my inquiries and sent photocopies of documents to me through the mail. Additionally, at this time, I began to piece together a bibliography of Murray's corpus of academic writing and to read (and reread) his work. Thus, Phase I of this project was largely exploratory as I expanded my knowledge of my subject by focusing on sources that were available to me, organized my nascent archive, and immersed myself in Murray's writing.

Phase II (2011–2017) began with my first visits to the Milne Special Collections and Archives at UNH in the winter of 2011, where I viewed Murray's teaching evaluations and assembled an account of his teaching schedule. Hearing the voices of Murray's students and gaining a bird's eye view of his yearly work was powerful in that it allowed me to begin to understand my subject in new ways, less as a famous person in our field and more as an English professor working in a college English department, much like myself. While researching at Milne I was also able to access and analyze a wide range of documents which shed light on the larger institutional context in which Murray operated at UNH as an undergraduate in the 1940s and, again, as a faculty member from the 1960s through the 1980s. In some ways, these documents carried me away from Murray, but they also helped paint a picture of the teaching of English at UNH in the twentieth century which ultimately helped me to understand the impact and influence of the university on Murray's intellectual and professional development. During Phase II I also gained access to a very haphazardly organized but ultimately productive departmental archive in the UNH English Department which shed further light on the local, institutional context of Murray's work. For much of Phase II, then, I pursued a series of new questions about UNH and its English department while still holding my questions about Murray close at hand. I also began to share the fruits of my labor, twice presenting papers at the Conference on College Composition and Communication (CCCC); publishing my first article about Murray (Michaud, "Victims, Rebels, and Outsiders"); publishing interviews with members of the UNH community who knew and worked with him (Michaud, "Democratizing Writing") and publishing a memoir about my own enculturation process into the UNH writing "tribe" (Michaud, *Notes of a Native Son*).

---

13   The world financial crisis caused Poynter to tighten its belt in the area of staffing and this meant, ultimately, suspending public access to Murray's materials.

Phase III of this project (2017–present) began on a warm spring morning in April 2017 when I first gained access to Murray's materials in a dark cinder block building on the outskirts of the UNH campus. A few weeks earlier I had received word that with the help of a generous donor, Murray's archive was coming home. That morning and on a series of subsequent trips, as I reviewed thousands of uncatalogued documents, my knowledge and understanding of my subject deepened as I connected dots across years of inquiry and finally began to conceptualize this book. I continued to publish during this time, as well, including additional interviews with members of the UNH family of teacher/scholar/writers (see Michaud, "Composing a Career"; "On the Creative-Nonfiction of Composition and Rhetoric") and retrospective pieces on the anniversary of two of Murray's major publications (Michaud, "What We Talk About When We Talk About Donald Murray"; Michaud and Downs). In sum, I have spent Phase III of this project among Murray's effects and at the writer's desk, trying to synthesize roughly a dozen years of research into something coherent, this book, *A Writer Reforms (The Teaching of) Writing*, the title of which nods playfully to Murray's first book of writing about writing, *A Writer Teaches Writing*, published just over a half century ago.

As to approach, I draw in these pages on a methodology called microhistory and I am indebted to Bruce McComiskey and the contributors to his excellent collection *Microhistories of Composition* for introducing me to this approach. Microhistory, with its emphasis on granular particularity and specificity, a reduction in the scale and scope of inquiry, and an embrace of nuance and complexity is well-suited to the work of rescuing, recovering, and reframing historical figures such as Donald Murray. According to Stock, microhistory accords "historical agency" to individuals by "avoiding labels based on preconceived norms" (194). According to Brian Gogan, microhistorical approaches encourage historians to "knock the rust off" "corroded" conceptual categories and "render more nuanced representation[s]" of disciplinary figures and forebears. In these pages, I aim for both, and a bit more. As the historian Edward Muir explains, microhistory offers an approach which seeks to understand "individuals making choices and developing strategies within the constraints of their own time and place" (Muir, qtd. in McComiskey 20). And therein lies my rationale in approaching Murray through the lens of the microhistory and the archive for what has been missing in much of the scholarship on Murray is a specific rendering of the choices he made and the strategies he developed within the constraints of *his* own time and place. This book aims to fill that void by hewing closely to the historical record and drawing extensively on primary documents to bring to life Murray's many contributions to our field's growth and development while also placing his work within the context of his personal story, his institutional affiliation with the University of New Hampshire, and his membership in the early, burgeoning modern field of composition and rhetoric.

In the pages that follow, I organize my investigation into Murray's life and work by attempting to answer two questions: *why*, after transitioning to college teaching in 1963, did Donald Murray work to reform the teaching of writing in schools (and schools themselves) and *how* did he go about this work? I begin, in Chapter 1, with the *why*, attending, first, to Murray's complex childhood as he, himself, narrated it in numerous memoirs and autobiographies and second, to his undergraduate years as an English major at UNH. Here, I attempt to understand how Murray's literacy narrative came to serve as an important exigence for his educational and disciplinary reform project once he transitioned to college teaching. In Chapters 2 through 4, I investigate the *how* of Murray's reform work. I begin, in Chapter 2, with an examination of the years 1963–1971, during which time Murray found himself unexpectedly working with two groups of students—freshman and pre-service teachers—who caused him to begin to theorize about composition pedagogy. These early experiences drew Murray into his first major reform project, a collaboration with a school administrator's organization, the New England School Development Council (NESDEC), which came to serve as an important early sponsor of his work. In Chapter 3, focused on the years 1971–1977, I examine several of Murray's important reform projects at UNH, including and especially his efforts to design and experiment with a new kind of college writing class, what he liked to call "a remedial class at an advanced level." I also examine his brief tenure as director of Freshman English, during which time he worked to reform the teaching of writing in general education at the university. In Chapter 4, I focus on the final decade or so of Murray's years on the faculty at UNH, 1977–1988, a period of amazing growth and innovation in the teaching and study of writing at the university and in the larger field beyond. Here, I examine Murray's relationship with his closest collaborator, Donald Graves, and investigate their work to establish the UNH Writing Laboratory and to create two new doctoral programs in literacy and composition and a national conference in composition pedagogy and research. Further, I examine Murray's efforts to reinvent and adapt his writing to the new landscape of publishing in the field as publication norms evolved during this period. Finally, in the conclusion, I analyze Murray's growing sense of disillusionment with and alienation from the field in the early years of his retirement and then briefly examine the role of his wife, Minnie Mae, in his work, trying to understand the nature of their decades-long collaborations. I close with a discussion of Murray's legacy and my sense of his most important contribution to our field: his efforts to democratize writing, to make writers out of not just teachers and students but all who seek to learn and improve at the craft.

CHAPTER 1.

ROOTS OF A REFORMER

I became a university teacher of writing more than thirty years ago with an unusual credential and obsession. I undervalued both. The credential might be described as reverse academic: I did badly in school, dropping out of high school twice and finally flunking out. While most of my colleagues, who had gold stars on their foreheads since kindergarten, could not understand why their students were not learning, even resisted learning, I could understand them; I had been there.

> – Donald Murray, *Instructor's Manual (Write to Learn)*

[E]ducation is geared up for sameness. We want our students to perform to the standards of other students, to study what we plan for them to study, and to learn from it what we or our teachers learned. Yet our students learn, at least in writing, if they experience difference. . . . We must learn to accept and delight in the difference we find in our students.

> – Donald Murray, "Writing and Teaching for Surprise"

Donald Murray's path to becoming an educational and disciplinary reformer was, by no means, preordained. Murray was an accidental reformer. In joining the faculty at UNH in 1963, he was motivated, principally, by practical considerations, mainly, by a desire to discover a more financially predictable means of putting food on his family's table. After graduating from UNH in 1948 Murray began his journalism career as a copy boy at *The Boston Herald* where he quickly climbed through the ranks. In 1954, he won a Pulitzer Prize for editorial writing at which time he left the *Herald* for *Time* magazine, where things did not go smoothly. He left *Time* after just two years,[14] and embarked on a new career as a freelance writer. For the next seven years he penned feature articles and stories for some of the most well-known general interest periodicals of the post-war

---

14   Murray describes his time at *Time* in various places in his professional correspondence and is consistent in explaining why things didn't work out. The reasons seem to have been both social/cultural and professional. In one instance he writes, "I went to *Time* Magazine, and it was worse than high school. I think I was fired. They made me a TV producer and I was so insulted I quit that day and started freelancing" (Donald Murray Personal Reflection). In another instance, of his time at *Time* he writes, "TURNING POINT: I wanted to be a writer. I accepted offer to work as a writer at *Time*. Bought a Victorian house at 380 Ridgewood Ave., Glen Ridge, New Jersey. *Time* was a cruel and destructive experience. I was fired in less than two years. Well I was made a TV producer when I wanted to write. I was out the door that morning." ("Donald Murray Revised Chronology").

era. By 1963, however, he was growing exhausted with the life of the writer-for-hire. When an offer to return to UNH to teach journalism arrived in the late fall of 1962, promising, in addition to a change of pace, those three essential middle-class entitlements to which Murray, a child of the working class, was especially susceptible, i.e., a steady paycheck, health insurance, and a retirement plan, he jumped at it.

In addition to personal motives, there were professional motivations at work as well in Murray's mid-life career transition—or, to be more precise, *writerly* motivations. Having published his first novel, *The Sensation*, in 1963, with the publication of a second, *The Man Who Had Everything*, forthcoming in 1964, and with a contract for a third novel in hand at the time when he received the offer from UNH, the opportunity to become a college English professor seemed to promise the time and space necessary for Murray to continue to pursue his ultimate goal: i.e., to write fiction free of the "commercial pressures" he lived under as a freelancer. In a 1962 letter to his agent Herb Jaffe, Murray muses, "[I]n my journalistic writing I am not doing the work I want to do, that I think I can do, and that I must at least try to do." He continues: "I feel I have something to say [and] I firmly believe this can be said best in fiction, particularly in novels. This is my first and foremost ambition, to write good fiction" ("Memorandum").[15]

The main thing to know, then, about the *why* of Donald Murray's reform efforts is that he did not set out in life to change the teaching of writing, the discipline of English, or the educational system. Nowhere in Murray's career trajectory leading up to the moment he returned to UNH to teach journalism do we find evidence of a desire to become a disciplinary and educational reformer. Why, then, did Murray swim with and not against the tide once he found himself in new and unanticipated waters during the early years of his second career? My reading in Murray's archive and especially in his autobiographical writing suggests that there were deep personal motivations at work in his decision to pursue a reform path once it revealed itself to him in the years 1963–1965.

In this chapter, in order to better understand these motivations, I first investigate what I call Murray's "literacy narrative," tracing his early experiences with reading, writing, and schooling growing up during the Great Depression in a working-class city south of Boston. In the stories Murray

---

15   Murray's first writerly goal, perhaps, was to become a famous poet. In 2006, the year of his death, he made a final revision to a chronological timeline he had started years earlier, based on a model he had seen in the book *The Seasons of a Man's Life*. In the entry for 1947, when Murray was 23 and a student at UNH, he writes: "Drove the laundry truck. Studied poetry only. No fiction or journalism. Was determined to be a poet."

tells about his school days, I find a clear exigence for his eventual decision to challenge the top-down, teacher-centered approach to education, in general, and the teaching of writing, in particular, that predominated across much of the K–16 system during this formative years. I then turn to examine his experiences as a student and, later, professor in the post-war UNH where, in the mainstream of the curriculum, composition and its teaching were relegated to second-class status. During this same era, however, within the extra-curriculum, Murray discovered and participated in an alternative disciplinary instantiation, one that placed writing (of the creative sort) and its teaching at English's center. In this way, Murray found at UNH during his student days a vision of the discipline to oppose and a vision to build upon and extend. He pursued both once he returned to join the faculty in 1963.

ROOTS OF A REFORMER, TAKE I

Throughout his second career Donald Murray thought and wrote a lot about schools, classrooms, and especially teachers—and about how they needed to change. He had good reason. Murray, who came of age during the Great Depression, attended school at a time when silence was seen as a virtue in a child and the classroom a place where teachers did all the talking. "I was trained under the rule that 'Children should be seen and not heard,'" Murray recalled late in his life. "We were hushed and not listened to; our opinions were not taken seriously. School was a place where we listened to the teacher who did not listen to us" (*Crafting a Life* 12). There was little Murray wanted to reform more, once he found himself in a position to do so, than the traditional relationship between students and teachers. This is signaled most powerfully by the fact that in his first book on writing, *A Writer Teaches Writing*, aimed at an audience not of writers or students but of *teachers*, Murray lists "He Listens" as the first of the seven skills teachers must learn in order to teach well. It was a profound reversal of role between teachers and students and one that challenged the very foundation upon which schools functioned. And it was Murray's foundational premise, a belief he sustained throughout his second career and an argument he hammered on without flagging: teachers must be people who listen.

Beyond reconsidering the relationship between teachers and students, Murray's school days struggles also led him to argue, as we see in the second epigraph above, that schools needed to become places that better accommodate difference and diversity. As he reports in numerous places in his corpus of work, Murray experienced the classrooms of his youth as places that cultivated sameness and conformity and refused to tolerate those who did not or could not fall in line. "My parents were told that I did not belong in school," he recalls in *A Writer*

Teaches Writing. "When I see how quickly and how permanently many of our students are evaluated, I cannot forget the years when I was told I was stupid, year after year, and I believed it" (160). It was not until much later in his life that Murray came to see his learning differences as strengths, but the fact that they led, in his youth, to academic struggle to the point that he eventually failed out of high school was not something he easily forgave, or forgot.[16]

In what follows, to better understand the personal exigencies driving Murray once he transitioned to college teaching, I reconstruct his literacy narrative,[17] investigating the autobiographical roots of what I consider to be his foremost reform goal: his advocacy for a new kind of teaching which emphasized listening over talking, receiving over sending, and responding over directing. Understanding Murray's literacy narrative is important for a few reasons. First, Murray, himself, saw his personal story as a central force guiding and motivating his reform work but rarely led with or mobilized it explicitly to make his arguments. In a late article, "All Writing is Autobiography," he writes, "I assume that many people in this audience are aware of my obsession with writing and my concern with teaching that began with my early discomfort in school that led to my dropping out and flunking out" (68). While some who knew Murray may well have been aware of his backstory, many, I am sure, did (and do) not. Second, Murray's failure to draw on his personal story may have come at a cost. As composition and rhetoric drew its attention to the politics of the classroom in the late 1980s and early 1990s, Murray was sometimes caricatured as an advocate of a feel-good, navel-gazing, politically disengaged approach to composition pedagogy. While this characterization is unfair, the fact is that Murray never confronted or responded to it, or, more to the point, mobilized his own personal story to speak back to it, as did others in the field at this time (see, for example Brodkey; Gilyard; Lu; Rose; Villanueva). Third, understanding Murray's literacy narrative is important because a receptive, listening, responding orientation towards students is, I believe, a foundational element of composition and rhetoric's ethos that distinguishes us from many other fields. We have Donald Murray, in part, to thank for this aspect of our disciplinary epistemology.

---

16   Given the lifelong challenges he faced with spelling, in particular, Murray speculated that he might have been partially dyslexic. An early report card and the marginal comments from a teacher in a collection of essays he wrote in first-year composition confirm that he had trouble with spelling throughout adolescence and into adulthood.

17   I am not the first or the only one to seek to better understand Murray's backstory and connect it to his work. In his article "Aloneness and the Complicated Selves of Donald Murray," Thomas J. Stewart mines Murray's autobiographical, outside-of-the-field writing to try to understand how his childhood experiences influenced his vision for writing pedagogy. Shane Combs, too, connects Murray's backstory to his teaching and approach.

~~~

Back Row, Sixth Grade

It is always October.
I trudge to school,
kick a stone, leap the crack
that goes to China,
take my seat in the back row, jam
my knees under the desk,
avoid chewing gum, waiting
for recess. The substitute
teacher hesitates
by the door. The bell
rings. She commands
attention to the text.
I cannot find my place.
There is no meaning
in the words. Nearsighted,
I squint at the blackboard:
The tails of dogs, a banana,
a winding river, a diving
hawk. I am in the wrong grade,
in a foreign school, another
century. I stare out the window,
learn how a robin drives a squirrel
from her nest, imagine
a fear of wings. Teacher
calls my name. I speak,
as surprised as if a bee
flew from my mouth.

– Donald Murray qtd. in *Crafting a Life* 111

I first encountered Murray's poem "Back Row, Sixth Grade" in his late-life book *Crafting a Life In Essay, Story, Poem.* He explains that it's a poem about education, underachieving students, about students with a case of attention deficit disorder, about day dreaming, about a shy student who didn't speak and therefore wasn't called on, about vision deprivation, about educational theory, educational psychology and a lot of other things. (112)

It's hard to read the poem or Murray's two memoirs, *My Twice-Lived Life: A Memoir* and *The Lively Shadow: Living with the Death of a Child* without thinking that he must have spent a good deal of his adult life trying to make peace with his early years—in *and* out of school. Born in 1924 in Quincy, Massachusetts, a member of the so-called "Greatest Generation," Murray was raised, by his own account, "in a double-decker behind an Amoco station on the trolley line" (*My Twice-Lived* 55). His father worked in the retail clothing business and by Murray's telling appears to have suffered from periodic but lifelong emotional and psychological instability. His mother was a homemaker who, according to Murray, exacted upon him forms of cruelty and abuse that were so severe that they are, at times, excruciating to read about. "I try to make peace with the past by reminding myself I live within a life that is so different from my childhood and so much better than I could ever have expected," Murray, age 72, wrote of his early life. "Still I am surprised at the continuing effort it takes to heal the hurts of a childhood lived so very many years ago, a past that is so painfully immediate today" (*Crafting a Life* 74).

A significant element of that pain stemmed from the silencing Murray reports having experienced as a boy—at home, at school, and on the playground—and the feelings of alienation and disempowerment such silencing engendered. Despite decades of writing and publishing prior to his transition to higher education, Murray did not begin to explore and share personal memories from his childhood in print until the mid to late 1970s, when he published an editorial, "Not-so-good-old-days," in a local New Hampshire newspaper. In this piece and again, later, in a chapter of the same title in his first memoir, *My Twice-Lived Life*, Murray shares and reflects on stories of the challenges he faced in school growing up.

> Many of my teachers taught as if they were doing time. It was the Great Depression, and perhaps that was a valid reason. They were imprisoned in their jobs, sometimes not paid, but still they hung on—for security.
>
> Most of my teachers were women who were forced to teach. I'm sympathetic to their predicament, but I don't romanticize the past. Few of my teachers had much interest in their subject, and most seemed to dislike or fear their students. ("Not-so-good-old days")

In the not-so-good-old-days, Murray recalls, "School was something to be survived" and few young people went on to college or were even expected to. "That was for the kids who lived on the hill. . . . The rest of us were not taken very seriously." The teaching methods of his youth were, Murray reports, organized primarily around rote learning. "We were ordered to memorize rules and information without any concept of their purpose or value. Ask 'Why?' and you got sent to the principal's office." Spelling bees, in Murray's memory, come in for special criticism. Such practices, he argues, allowed "children who knew how to spell [to] practice what they already knew while the rest of us failed in the first round or the second, sat down and glowered at them" ("Not-so-good-old days").

Murray's memories of teachers in the not-so-good-old-days were largely negative. "I hated all but three teachers between kindergarten and graduate school," he wrote in a *Boston Globe* column published late in his life ("The Past" C3). In high school, Murray reports, he failed out, in large part because of the incompetence and arrogance of his teachers, which he describes at length in *My Twice-Lived Life*:

> My English teacher in high school punished me in the eleventh and twelfth grades when she found out I had read ahead of the daily assignment, as I always did, usually reading the whole book the first night. My music teacher argued that Rimsky-Korsakov was a team like Gilbert and Sullivan. My art teacher made me use crosses for eyes. My guidance teacher gave me a B+ for a course in the eleventh grade I never attended. A history teacher jumped me between floors because I was a Scot and therefore on England's side. He was Irish and on Hitler's side. When I had the same chemistry and physics teacher in the last two years of high school, he never told me that a kid from my part of town could buy a slide rule. I got Ds on five-question daily quizzes when I answered one or two questions with hand-scrawled arithmetic, while the kids with slide rules clicked their way to A's. When I did get a slide rule in twelfth grade I was so far behind, I never figured it out—and there was no one at home who had ever seen such a contraption. (132)

Beyond his teachers, Murray recalls the suffering he experienced at the hands of his classmates, as well. On the playground he felt silenced by his peers—by their religious prejudices and the masculine norms of the day. "Each year of school, from first grade until sixth, I played the role of victim or Christian martyr," Murray writes (*My Twice-Lived Life* 24). He did so, he explains, because of the repeated violence he experienced at the hands of schoolyard bullies.[18] "Mother had told me that if I truly believed in Jesus Christ, the bully's hand would be stayed," Murray recalls. "I didn't believe hard enough; the bully's knuckles connected." "At school," he writes, "I hated the classroom and the playground" (*My Twice-Lived Life* 65).

While my focus here is on Murray's struggles in school, the challenges he faced at home, where he was an only child in a house full of apparently troubled adults, only exacerbated those he experienced at school. "I was a sickly child," he reports, "brought up in a hell-fire and brimstone house where eternal damnation sat waiting on the back porch, and I started each morning by going in to see if my grandmother, paralyzed by a stroke, had survived the night. My father was not happy with his job, my mother with her lot" (*The Literature of Tomorrow* 226). In his later life, Murray wrote at length about his parents in his columns and memoirs. His father, he explains, was "a hypochondriac all his life, taking to bed with illnesses real and imagined. He was in the retail business, dealing with women's fashions, and when his buying didn't match his customer's purchasing, he would take to his bed" (*My Twice-Lived Life* 64). Murray's mother, he confesses, "should never have been a mother. She had no talent for it and took no pleasure in it" (11).[19] In a short essay written late in his life, of his relationship with his mother Murray writes, "I cannot have the mother I wanted any more than she could have had the son of her expectations. I still hunger for that one conversation we can never have over a cup of orange pekoe tea at the red checked oilskin kitchen tablecloth and hear her express love for her only and offer respect for our mutual differences" ("Reading What I Haven't Written" 8).

To escape the suffering he experienced at home and school, Murray immersed himself in work and odd jobs. At his memorial service in 2007 Thomas Newkirk described Murray's early life as "molded from a Horatio Alger dime novel." Murray's own descriptions of his early years only confirm this observation. In a lovely passage in his memoir *The Lively Shadow*, Murray recalls the numerous occupations of his youth:

> A morning and afternoon and Sunday paper route; shoveling snow; performing hated yard work; serving as a shabbas [sic] goy the one year we lived in an Orthodox Jewish neighborhood; organizing a real estate office; restoring antiques,

---

18   Murray was a Scottish Baptist whereas many of his schoolmates in Quincy, Massachusetts were, as he tells it, Irish-Catholics.

19   Murray relates numerous painful anecdotes about his mother in his memoirs, including a story about the time when he returned home from the war to find that, assuming he would die and never return, she had sold or given away his clothing and belongings.

cutting wood, and building a chapel during the four summers
I was a "scholarship boy" at summer camp; making Scots
sausage at Miller's Market, where I also kept track of canned
goods inventory, decorated the store windows, and stacked
and sold fruit and vegetables, delivering with the store's truck
before I had a truck license; serving as chauffeur for the state
treasurer while I was in high school; cooking; house paint-
ing; unloading the inventory for the first supermarket in my
neighborhood; quitting school in the spring of my tenth,
eleventh, and twelfth grades to work on the Boston Record
and American—all showed that getting to work early, running
when others walked, and staying late could not earn me love
but did produce respect—and money. (127–28)

As this passage suggests, work gave Murray things he could not get from
school or at home—self-worth, pride, and meaning. "Work, not religion, was
my salvation," he recalls (*The Lively Shadow* 127). When he wasn't working he
pursued the life of the mind, feeding his inexhaustible only-child's curiosity
with self-sponsored artistic and literate activity. He was, he writes, "a compul-
sive reader far beyond my grade level, a child artist, a scholar in my own way of
topics that interested me" (*The Lively Shadow* 127). Outside of school, Murray
recalls, he was "learning on my own at a mad pace, gulping down a half dozen
books or more every week." He continues:

I cannot remember when I could not read and did not spend
part of every day reading. My curiosity took me through the
children's shelves of the Wollaston branch library to the adult
sections, where I was not supposed to read but did, and on
to the huge main Thomas Crane Library in Quincy, Massachusetts, where I started making notes for one of the books I
published a lifetime later. I was learning all the time—on the
street, at work, at home and church and summer camp—but
not in school. (*My Twice Lived Life* 129)

In school, as we have seen, Murray was taught to see himself as *not-a-learner*.
"I thought I was stupid" he recalls, and eventually came to accept "the docu-
mented fact that I was stupid" even though he "was placed in the highest level of
a thirteen-track system because of [his] IQ tests" (*My Twice-Lived Life* 129–32).
School was "something to escape" and so, not surprisingly, Murray dropped out
of high school twice before eventually failing out in the 12th grade (*My Twice-
Lived Life* 133–34). At this point he enrolled at the Tilton School, a private

boarding academy in New Hampshire, where he was a "scholarship boy," his tuition, room, and board paid for by a football scholarship and a job as a resident assistant. After a year at Tilton, Murray graduated and was then drafted into the army where he served in the European theater during World War II.

It was not until he arrived home from war and enrolled as an English major at UNH in the winter of 1946 that Murray finally experienced school in a way that was less about silence and its attendant feelings of embarrassment, humiliation, and shame and more about voice and the feelings which accompany it: pride, empowerment, and a sense of authority. His recollections of his undergraduate years at UNH in the 1940s are imbued with memories of talk, conversation, and dialogue. "Looking back," he recalls, "I realize how much I was changed by those fast-passing, jam-packed months of reading and writing and talking, always talking" ("To Heck with Nostalgia" 9). While talking was, as Murray recalls, a significant part of the experience at UNH, so was listening, and it was the act of *being listened to* by his professors that seems to have resonated with him the most. "We were learning because our professors were learning with us," Murray writes, summoning the unique post-war environment in which world-wise veterans forced their way into university classrooms and challenged the authority of their professors. "They didn't lecture so much as challenge us to read and criticize," Murray writes. "When we did, they gave us the complement of listening and the greater compliment of counter-attack—heated, personal, and caring. My teachers in Durham taught me to respect and listen to the individual student, to delight in diversity, to be myself and reveal my feelings as well as my opinions honestly" ("To Heck with Nostalgia" 9–10).

While it wasn't roses all the way down, as we will see in the next section, Murray does seem to have experienced, during his years as an undergraduate English major at UNH, a pedagogy rooted in the importance of listening to and encouraging student autonomy and authority. Most importantly, though, his professors were able to encourage him, after so many years of educational disenfranchisement and alienation, to trust that the things he had to say had value and worth in the world and that he had a right and even an obligation to say them. James A. Herrick, a scholar of the history and theory of rhetoric, has written eloquently about the importance of voice, the danger of silence. "When speech is viewed as the characteristic human capacity, to deny speech by silence is to deny one's humanity," he argues (174). Feeling that his humanity had been denied by the teachers of his youth, Donald Murray focused his educational reform efforts once he transitioned to college teaching on working to ensure that the humanity of his students (and future generations of students) would be encouraged, and that their voices would be heard.

ROOTS OF A REFORMER, TAKE II

In the last section, having traced the struggles and challenges Donald Murray reports haveing experienced in school and at home in his youth, I suggested that his time as an undergraduate English major at UNH in the 1940s was significant in that he found, in the exuberant classrooms of the early post-war era, professors who allowed him to experience education as a form of empowerment and who listened to and encouraged him to develop and exercise his voice. As we saw above in Murray's 1987 essay "To Heck with Nostalgia," he recalled with enthusiasm and gratitude the "fast-passing, jam-packed months of reading and writing and talking" he experienced at UNH under the leadership of faculty who made such meaningful engagement with schooling and literacy possible. "To Heck with Nostalgia," however, was written for UNH's alumni magazine, where encomiums to professors are the norm and the old alma mater is always cast in a positive light. Elsewhere in Murray's corpus of work and in his archive there is evidence of a more complicated relationship with his UNH mentors or, if not with them, exactly, with what they represented as local instantiations of the mid-twentieth century discipline of English. This second story contains significant implications for understanding Murray and his work, for what has been obscured by the *Donald Murray = Expressivist* frame, or just forgotten entirely, are the many arguments Murray advanced in the field for the disciplinary reform of English as well as the vital role he played in helping the emergent modern field of composition and rhetoric develop and articulate an identity separate from English. If Murray's educational reform efforts were grounded in his childhood experiences of personal and academic struggle and even trauma, his attempts to reform the discipline of English can be traced, in part, to his experiences as an undergraduate English major and, later, faculty member at UNH (in the only college English department he ever knew from the inside). The mid-twentieth century discipline of English as Murray experienced at UNH offered him a vision of the discipline to challenge and push back against *and* a tradition to build on and extend. Once he was in a position to do so as a faculty member, he would pursue both paths.

Liberal Culture at "A Poor Man's College"

As Sharon Crowley has argued, "around 1971" English teachers and scholars in U.S. secondary schools and colleges and universities began to work to reform the way writing was taught within English departments and what we have come to think of as the writing process movement got underway. "A large body of textual evidence attests," Crowley writes, "that a pedagogical turn . . . was widely recommended in professional literature during the late 1960s and throughout the 1970s" (187). Crowley sources Murray's 1972 article "Teach Writing as a Process Not Product" to support her claims, but it's important to note that by 1972 Murray had already been working to reform the teaching of English (and writing within it) for almost a decade, and one of his key arguments, borne out of that experience, actually preceded the claim for teaching process. The warrant for the assertion that teachers of English should teach process not product is the argument that writing is, in the first place, among the sorts of things that *are* teachable and therefore learnable—by all students. This warrant, as Murray well knew, was not one upon which all teachers and professors of English, including his mid-twentieth colleagues at UNH, agreed.

While Murray had obviously gained exposure to English in the many years of his schooling leading up to his enrollment at UNH, his decision to declare his undergraduate major as English signaled an ambition to commit himself more seriously to the discipline. What he could not and likely did not know, however, was that the UNH English Department was, in the very year of his matriculation at the university, 1946, embarking on a new concentrated program of study grounded in what Berlin has dubbed "the rhetoric of liberal culture" (*Rhetoric and Reality* 43). For most of the UNH English Department's first epoch, which ran from roughly 1912–1946,[20] the program in English had been largely pragmatic in nature. Study in English, as one catalogue put it, was seen as a means of "preparation for many varieties of work after college" (*Bulletin 1945–46* 115). In this way, the epoch one English major at UNH was well-suited to students enrolling in what was, to borrow a phrase from the school's first institutional historian, Donald Babcock, "a poor man's college" (221). The English curriculum was notable for its diversity, inclusivity, and usefulness—*diverse* in that it included many areas of language study from which students could choose, *inclusive* in that each area counted towards fulfillment of graduation requirements for the major, and *useful* in that the coursework, including classes in literary studies, was designed and marketed to speak to students' vocational aspirations.

The revision of this pragmatic, student-centered program of study began in earnest in the 1920s and 1930s as the faculty at the New Hampshire College of

---

20 The department was founded as the Department of English and Psychology in 1903 but did not take on a clear sense of professional identity until 1912 and 1913 when Dr. Alfred Richards and Mr. Harold Scudder, respectively, joined the faculty. Richards guided the department as chair until his retirement in 1939, at which point Scudder took over, serving until 1946 when he, too, retired. Together, these two men, a Yale Ph.D. trained in philology and a Dartmouth A.B. trained as a newspaperman and public relations specialist, shaped the vision of English at UNH during the department's first epoch.

Agriculture and the Mechanic Arts, as of 1923 the University of New Hampshire, began to professionalize. Within English, a cohort of Yale-trained scholars with doctorates in literature began to arrive around this time and quickly got to work reshaping the major.[21] As Berlin has noted, Yale and Princeton were "the primary centers" of liberal culture in the late-nineteenth and twentieth centuries (*Rhetoric and Reality* 72). As such, and to varying degrees, faculty who received their training at these institutions carried with them the liberal culture ethos as they ventured out to less well-heeled colleges and universities to spread the liberal culture project and instill in their charges an education that was "aristocratic and humanistic," while immersing them in "traditional learning of literature, language, and art" (*Rhetoric and Reality* 43). The goal, as Berlin reminds us, was the production of a particular kind of subjectivity, that of an "aristocrat who demonstrated his education through living a certain kind of life" (*Rhetoric and Reality* 39).

The ways in which faculty trained at schools like Yale and Princeton worked to impose the liberal culture project on students at schools like UNH can be glimpsed in the changes initiated in the UNH English Department in the 1930s and 1940s. These began in earnest in 1935, when prerequisite courses for the major, which had previously focused equally on writing, reading, and speaking, were re-oriented to center *only* on literary study (*Bulletin 1935–36* 161–62). It continued in 1939, when the English Department abolished the freshman composition program and allowed students who earned a sufficient score on a writing entrance examination to proceed directly to coursework in literature (those who didn't score high enough were enrolled in remedial tutorials in basic composition)[22] (Scudder, "A Functional" 413–15; Scudder & Webster, "The New Hampshire Plan" 493–95). And it reached its zenith in 1946 when Dr. Sylvester Bingham, himself a Yale man, ascended to department chair and oversaw the creation of a new English curriculum which foregrounded the study of literature and liberal culture as "understanding and appreciation of the thought of the great minds of the past" (*Bulletin 1945–46* 98–99). An exit examination tied to graduation was instituted at this time, as well, to test students' understanding and appreciation of the western literary and cultural tradition. In sum, if, during the UNH English Department's first epoch, the English major was student-centered, with faculty allowing *students* to decide what a degree in English entailed, during the department's second epoch, which I pin to the years

---

21   The association between Yale's English department and UNH's can be traced to the arrival on the faculty, in 1911, of Dr. Alfred Richards, who earned his A.B. in English from Yale in 1898.

22   Freshman English was re-established a half-dozen years later, in 1946, as part of a general education revision, under the leadership of chairman Sylvester Bingham.

1946–1968, it was *faculty* who determined what the study of English would involve and it would involve, principally, the study of western literature and liberal culture.[23]

THE MAKING OF A "WRITER'S UNIVERSITY"

While the teaching of writing within the mainstream of the English curriculum at UNH during the post-war years was subordinated to the teaching of literature and liberal culture a different tradition existed in the extracurriculum, one which placed writing of the "creative" sort (and its teaching), at the discipline's center. As Katherine Tirabassi has shown in her award-winning dissertation, beginning in the 1930s and under the charismatic leadership of Dr. Carroll Towle, UNH became, through several inspired extracurricular initiatives, a "writer's university." Like Dr. Bingham and other members of the epoch two faculty, Towle received his doctorate from Yale, where he studied sixteenth and seventeenth century British literature. He began to teach writing classes at UNH shortly after his arrival in 1931,[24] creating his long-running and much memorialized course, Writing as an Art, in 1935, described thus in the UNH *Bulletin* that year:

> A course in the study and practice of the forms of writing through an examination of the history of literary criticism. The reading of famous critical essays and of many contemporary opinions, correlated with practice writing of various types. Each student is allowed to spend much of his time with the type he finds most congenial. (*Bulletin 1935–36* 166–67)

As D. G. Myers has argued, instruction in creative writing of the sort Towle offered at UNH in the 1930s was typical of its era, having recently emerged in U.S. schools and colleges and universities as an alternative to more culturally or humanistically-oriented approaches to the teaching of English. Over time, Writing as an Art narrowed its focus to center less on the consumption of "famous

---

23   This top-down, faculty-centered program of study eventually created strains for the department as students began to shy away from the major. In the eyes of department chair Bingham, however, the cause of the drop in the number of English majors was more the result of the mediocre caliber of students being admitted to the university. "If plans are not made now for the raising of admission requirements or, at least, the enforcement of the present ones," Bingham complains in a memo to the liberal arts dean in the summer of 1958, "the University will be inundated with mediocrity" (Bingham).

24   Dr. Claude Lloyd first offered instruction in creative writing at UNH in the 1920s in his course on the short story. Towle picked up the mantle of this work following Lloyd's departure in the early 1930s. (*Bulletin 1928–29,* 142)

and critical essays" and more on the production of writing that students found "most congenial." Here, for example, is a description of the course from 1946, the year Murray took it with Towle:

> The study and practice of forms of writing, together with an examination of the history of literary philosophy. Practice in mutual criticism through class workshop discussions and written comment. Freedom in selection and pursuance of writing interests. Individual conferences. (*Bulletin 1945–46* 212)

As we learn from Tirabassi, Towle was the driving force behind the rich extracurricular writing culture that existed at UNH from the late 1930s until his sudden death in 1962 (one year, it's worth noting, before Murray returned to join the faculty). Most significantly Towle was the founder and director of the UNH Summer Writer's Conference (1938–1962), which was ranked among the "Big Four" such conferences nationally (Tirabassi 175). Held each August and attracting more than 100 writers and writing teachers from around the country, the conference was unique in that it was open to a wide range of participants and not just practicing or professional writers. As successful as it was, however, Towle argued that the conference did not so much *create* UNH's writing reputation as it built on and extended it. By the time the first conference was held in 1938, UNH students had already been publishing a successful literary journal, *The Student Writer*, and winning regional and national writing competitions for almost a decade.

Students and UNH community members were also able to engage in UNH's rich extracurricular writing culture during these years via participation in a home-grown initiative sponsored by Towle, The Folio Club, an informal gathering of students, teachers, and professional writers who met at Towle's home in Durham to discuss writing. At Folio Club meetings participants shared and critiqued one another's work and read and discussed contemporary American literature, which was, at this time, only just beginning to gain a foothold in the mainstream of the curriculum in the UNH English Department. In sum, from the student literary journal to the annual writer's conference, from writing prizes to the Folio Club, UNH came to be, during the pre- and post-war years, an important site in the practice, teaching, and cultivation of (creative) writing and Dr. Towle was instrumental in this process, championing, in Tirabassi's words, "The notion that student writers should be considered as potential contributors to the emergent contemporary American literary sensibility" (132).

As we saw in the second description of Writing as an Art, above, and as we learn from accounts of Towle's teaching in the campus newspaper, he engaged in a range of progressive pedagogies that would soon become staples of "process" pedagogy (e.g., providing students with the chance to explore and experiment with different genres of writing, allowing students to choose their own topics, encouraging students to develop and improve their work through an iterative revision process, creating opportunities for students to share work-in-progress with peers). At a time when some in the UNH English Department believed that writing was the result of inspired genius and therefore largely unteachable, Towle worked to create an egalitarian teaching and learning environment in which any student could learn what he called "the art of expression in language" (*An Anthology* vi–vii). Here, for example, is Towle in the student newspaper circa 1941, guiding students in submitting work for the annual *Atlantic Monthly* writing contests (numerous UNH students won these contests, including Donald Murray):

> In view of the fine opportunities offered and the comparative success of New Hampshire writers in the past, I urge everyone who thinks that he possesses any ability [in writing] to give serious attention to the thought of contributing one or more entries [to this year's contests]. I shall be glad to talk with or assist anyone in putting his manuscript in readiness for competition. ("Literary Contests" 4)

As this passage illustrates, Dr. Towle welcomed all comers to the writer's table. Of his inclusive pedagogical approach, Tirabassi, who studied his papers extensively, writes,

> Although some of the [writing] initiatives [under Towle] had some small requirement to gain access . . . most . . . placed few restrictions, if any, on membership or participation. In all cases, the themes and topics discussed focused on the present moment—offering participants an opportunity to create, to write, to discuss writing-in-process with peers, professors, and published writers, to provide feedback to other writers, to study popular culture, and to read texts that were not yet "appropriate" in the formal curriculum. The emphasis on informality, open access and contemporary themes seem to be features that differentiate these initiatives from the formal curriculum at UNH. (166)

In sum, in the extracurriculum at UNH during the middle years of the 20th century Dr. Carroll Towle established an alternative tradition of English upon which Donald Murray and others could and would later build. It was a tradition that existed largely outside of the department's central disciplinary vision but existed, nonetheless, gaining for UNH a reputation in the production and teaching of (creative) writing. When Murray became a faculty member at UNH in the early sixties, he very much saw himself as working within this tradition, as he explains in the following passage:

> New Hampshire was for me a place of teachers and learning and books and writing, especially writing. I joined a community of men and women who were writers, or who dreamed of being writers. . . . Now, on some days Carroll Towle's son, David, sits across my desk talking about his writing as I sat across his father's desk talking about my writing. . . .
>
> Most mornings I sit at my desk looking out at New Hampshire woods trying to do what my teachers taught me. Most afternoons I meet with my students trying to pass on my teachers' lessons of craft. New Hampshire has become more than a place; it is a way of working which gives me a personal sense of continuity—lessons taught and lessons continually learned. ("City Boy Finds Woods" A31)

CONCLUSION

Why would a Pulitzer Prize-winning writer who had successfully placed articles and stories in the most-well known publications of his day and who had published two novels and had a third under contract decide, over the span of just a few years, to throw virtually all of his prodigious energy behind an unanticipated new mission? My answer to this question has been my argument in this chapter: Donald Murray's efforts to reform schools were grounded in his frustrated childhood of educational struggle and failure. His work trying to reform the field of English was rooted in his feelings of frustration and even anger about the way writing and its teaching was marginalized within the discipline as he had experienced it at UNH. While I have never found evidence that Murray consciously set out to pursue reform as a primary goal prior to his return to UNH in 1963, once drawn into a reform current during his early years in the classroom Murray swam with the tide, and kept swimming with it, for the rest of his life. Having examined, in this chapter, the personal forces driving Murray's reform project(s), the *why* of his reform, I turn, now, to investigate its *how*, sharing what I've learned about the numerous efforts Murray made to change both English and the schools in which it was taught during the second half of his career.

CHAPTER 2.
BECOMING A WRITER TEACHING WRITING, 1963–1971

There are some people, writers included, who do not think that the testimony of writers should be taken seriously. They believe that the artist works dumbly, not knowing what he is doing. I believe that the artist is first of all a craftsperson and knows a great deal of what is being done during the act of writing. I think that a careful study of how writers write reveals significant information.

– Donald Murray, A *Writer Teaches Writing*, 2nd ed.

[The] process by which successful writers have brought their work to its final form has not been the interest of the pedagogue. Rather has he dissected the finished product—and from such analysis he has delivered to inarticulate students counsels of literary perfection.

– Raymond Weaver, qtd. in Berlin *Rhetoric and Reality*

I was hired at the age of 39 as a teacher and I didn't know how to teach. I looked at the textbooks—one of them was the Fowler approach and things like this. I read a good many of the books on the train between Durham and Boston at the time in the summer. I came here in July and I was going to teach in September and they made no sense at all, any more than my high school and college texts had. They were written by people who didn't write, and if you followed their instructions, you'd write badly.

– Donald Murray, "A Conversation About the Writing Craft with Don Murray"

I like to imagine a young(ish) Donald Murray in the summer of 1963, riding the train back and forth between Durham, New Hampshire and Boston, contemplating his mid-life career change as what we have come to think of as "the Sixties" was getting underway. Murray, 39, had a wife and three kids to think about as he rode the rails to a new life in a place that was not new, at least to him. In signing on at UNH, he had agreed to uproot his family from the comfortable upper-middle class suburbs of northern New Jersey where they had settled, surrender the large Victorian home that stood as a symbol of all his professional success, and, by his account, forfeit roughly half of his annual salary. Most significantly, though, he had chosen to embark on a new career for which he had no formal training, background, or experience, and to take on a new professional identity, *teacher*, which must have stirred up at least some demons from his past.

As we learned in the last chapter, Murray's decision to become a college English professor was motivated by both practical and professional considerations. A profile published in the UNH campus newspaper at the start of his second year on campus confirms his initial plan to pursue his dream of becoming a fiction writer: "I [first] came to the University as an out-of-state student because of the artistic climate created by Carroll [Towle]," Murray explains in the article. "I came back to enjoy the same climate" ("I Have to Write" 10). The photo that accompanies the piece conveys a sense of Murray's writerly persona at the time. Seated in his home office, feet up on a desk, a tower of five-inch-thick binders containing the manuscript of his first novel, *The Man Who Had Everything,* on a table nearby, Murray is the very image of the mid-twentieth century American novelist.

As he points out in the epigraph at the start of this chapter, however, Murray's most immediate task that summer of 1963 was to learn how to teach, and to teach journalism, specifically. Since there were so few such courses on the books for him to teach at this time, however, he was forced to become a teacher of other kinds of writing, as well, and, just as important, of other kinds of students. It was because of Murray's experiences teaching writing and students beyond journalism that he was drawn into a new and unanticipated role during the early to mid 1960s, *reformer*, an identity he would try, at times, in the years that followed, to shake but which, eventually, would come to define him for the entirety of the second half of his career (and into his retirement).

In this chapter, I explore the early years of Murray's transition from writer-for-hire to writer-teaching-writing. Having examined, in the last chapter, the *why* of his journey, I begin, in this chapter, to investigate the *how*. How did Murray become a reformer? And how did he go about his reform work (and with whom)? In what follows I focus, first, on Murray's work on campus, at UNH, teaching Freshman English and Expository Writing, the latter a class for pre-service English teachers. I then turn to examine his work away from campus and, in particular, his collaborations with an important early sponsor, the New England School Development Council (NESDEC), which gave him access to a broader audience of practicing teachers with whom to experiment and test his emergent ideas about composition pedagogy. Murray's earliest reform work can, as we will see, be situated within James Zebroski's claim that "The origin of most of the key ideas in composition and rhetoric from 1968 to 1980 came from those associated with schools of education or with teacher education" (29). While the origin of many of Murray's earliest ideas about composition and rhetoric stemmed from his experience as a practicing, professional writer or from his reading in the testimonial literature of writers and journalists, his work in teacher education at UNH and beyond provided the opportunity to begin to think critically about composition pedagogy during his early years in the field and develop his own unique approach.

EARLY INTERVENTIONS WITH "THE PEDAGOGUE"

In keeping with the typical teaching load of English faculty members at UNH during the early 1960s, Murray taught four courses per semester in his first years back on campus. His primary responsibility was a news writing course, but he also taught two service classes—Freshman English and Expository Writing, the latter a newly-created advanced composition course for pre-service teachers which, according to Murray, had gone unstaffed prior to his arrival "because of English department snobbery about methods courses" (*My Twice-Lived Life* 137). Given how little else there was for Murray to teach at this time, he signed on for Expository Writing despite the fact that he had no advanced graduate training in English or education, no experience working with pre-service teachers, and was, himself, a high school dropout.

As he explains in two summative reports written to department chair Bingham during his first year, Murray found the work in Expository Writing gratifying beyond expectation. The class, he declares with enthusiasm in his report on the fall semester (1963), was his "most successful," its success being measurable in the "evolution of the papers" his students wrote and their ability to operationalize his primary objective: "to make the student experience the craft of writing" (Murray, Report on First Semester). In his spring semester report (1964), and despite the fact that he hadn't taught the course again that term, Murray returns to ruminate on his experience in expository writing, explaining that it was, of all the classes he taught his first year, "the course in which, I believe, I teach the most about my craft" (Murray, Report on Second Semester).

As we also learn from Murray's spring semester report, it wasn't just the experience of teaching Expository Writing that was revelatory, however. It was the experience of teaching Expository Writing and Freshman English *simultaneously* that was so impactful for him. Filled as it was with students who were only marginally interested in learning to write, Freshman English was the ideal "laboratory," as Murray put it, in which he could "test out the techniques" about "the craft of writing" he was teaching his future teachers in Expository Writing. In sum, Murray's unanticipated work with first-year students in Freshman English and pre-service English teachers in Expository Writing provided an important early opportunity to begin to theorize about composition pedagogy—and to realize that he found such work meaningful, even fun.

Of what did Murray's early theorizing consist? His reports to Dr. Bingham offer some clues. In his fall report, he shares his concern about the quantity of writing students were asked to produce in Freshman English. Murray apparently felt that an important aspect of composition pedagogy was sheer practice, of which, it seems, he believed students were not getting enough. Of his experience teaching Freshman English, a class with a heavily proscribed curriculum, standardized syllabus, and limited set of assignments, Murray writes, "I feel it is important that students be given the opportunity to write." Again, later, he writes, "The student can only learn to write if he writes." His Freshman English students, he reports, wrote seventeen short pieces during the semester (the standardized syllabus specified that they only need write ten). His Expository Writing students wrote fourteen. "I do not feel that the number of papers required from an individual student can be cut," Murray writes in the conclusion of his fall report. "In fact, I intend to increase it wherever possible. . . . The quality of their work depends directly on its quantity." Thus, frequent opportunities for practice seems to have been an important early element of Murray's approach to composition pedagogy (Murray, Report on First Semester). He would later operationalize this belief by implementing a weekly five-page writing requirement in many of the writing courses he taught.

In Murray's reports to Bingham circa 1963 and 1964, we also see the kernel of what would later become a central tenet of his method: his belief that to improve at writing students must learn and experience what the practicing, publishing writer knows and not just write assignments to satisfy the teacher. "I want to place a challenge before those students who study writing with me," Murray writes in his fall report. "I want them to experience the craft of writing and rewriting. I want them to approximate whenever possible the job of the professional writer." That job, as Murray understood it, was one of identifying and solving the myriad problems that arise for the writer during the act of composing. In this way, Murray conceived of writing as a kind of problem-solving activity—for himself and his students. "I believe that my teaching has a vitality because I am solving the same problems of writing which face the student," he explains, and therein lies a third additional important element of Murray's early theorizing about composition pedagogy: writing teachers and writing students are on the same plane, trying to solve similar kinds of problems and, engaged, essentially, in the same task (Murray, Report on First Semester).

MAKING WRITERS OF TEACHERS

As I suggested earlier, Murray's earliest work in what was at this time barely an academic field can be situated within accounts published by composition historians who, with Patricia Stock, have argued that collaboration with K–12 teachers was foundational to the growth and development of composition and rhetoric from the 1960s through the 1990s. While Murray was not a member of a school or college of education he was drawn, as we have seen, into teacher education via his involvement in the expository writing course at UNH. In his report to Dr. Bingham on his second semester in the classroom, Murray describes his preparations for teaching the course again the next fall and how "in order to make it a more effective course for teachers," he had visited a number of area high schools to try to better understand how writing was being taught in English classrooms of the day. In this way, Murray was drawn further out of his writer's study and away from his writer's desk and into the world of K–12 education. Then, during his second year at UNH he had another experience which drew him out and away even further (Murray, Report on Second Semester).

Zebroski argues that the "social formation" that became contemporary composition studies was largely a "bottom[s] up" undertaking, created not by, or not *just* by, professors of college English but, rather, by what he dubs "early informal, unstable, often antidisciplinary collectives of people" who were engaged, in one way or another, with the task of teacher education (29). As I've argued above, Murray's work during his first years in the profession can be situated within this claim, with his most significant early engagement in the kinds of "collectives" Zebroski describes beginning in the fall of 1964, when he gave a public lecture on writing in Hollis, New Hampshire that led to a multi-year collaboration with NESDEC. A regional professional association for school administrators, NESDEC, not exactly an "antidisciplinary collective," was a key early partner for Murray, who was all too happy to provide the antidisciplinarianism. Its executive secretary, Richard Goodman, formerly the superintendent of schools in Hollis and the person to whom Murray dedicates the first edition of *A Writer Teaches Writing*, was concerned with improving the teaching of writing in K–12 education and so was interested in Murray's efforts to devise new approaches to composition pedagogy.[25] From 1964–1971, under Goodman's leadership, NESDEC served as Murray's most important collaborator and sponsor, validating his authority and expertise and giving him a platform from which to speak. If Murray's early work at UNH in Expository Writing had given him access to a small audience of future teachers to influence and educate in his emergent writer-based approach to composition pedagogy, his work with NESDEC offered him access to a much larger audience of practicing teachers with whom to further develop his ideas, approach, and arguments. If, as Raymond Weaver puts it in

25   Murray's dedicatory note to Goodman reads: "This book is dedicated to Dick Goodman who must accept full responsibility for luring the author into the maze of elementary and secondary education."

the epigraph at the start of this chapter, "[The] process by which successful writers have brought their work to its final form has not been the interest of the pedagogue," Murray, with NESDEC's help, would try to make it so.[26]

Murray's work with NESDEC got underway in 1964 when he penned a professional development proposal for a program to "improve the teaching of composition in secondary schools" by applying "the experience of the professional writer to the teaching of composition in the high school." The idea, as Murray explains it, was "To encourage the student to approach the task of composition in the same way that the writer does his job" (Preliminary memorandum). Following this first proposal Murray soon got to work on a short pamphlet entitled *What a Writer Does,* to set down, for the first time, his philosophy and method of composition pedagogy. The plan was that NESDEC would publish *What a Writer Does* and distribute it to members of its teacher network and Murray would use the pamphlet as an instructional aid during professional development workshops and seminars with NESDEC teachers. As the pamphlet evolved, however, eventually expanding into *A Writer Teaches Writing,* so did Murray's work with NESDEC. In the summer of 1967, he designed and led a first-ever summer professional development workshop for teachers at Bowdoin College at which he and a small cohort of NESDEC instructors initiated attendees in Murray's emergent writer-based approach to composition pedagogy. This work continued for three more summers, giving Murray the chance to interact with and learn from and about practicing school teachers.[27]

Beyond directing summer workshops Murray expanded his professional development work with NESDEC during the 1967–68 academic year when he taught his first graduate course, Writing and the Teaching of Writing, at NESDEC's headquarters in Cambridge, Massachusetts. Here an important change in his approach to professional development took place as he shifted away from trying to tell teachers about what writers do (as he had done at Bowdoin) and towards trying to make writers of teachers. At the first Bowdoin workshop in

---

26   Weaver was among several English professors who argued for the benefits of having professional writers work with writing teachers. In a post-mortem on the 1962 Project English summer conferences, Erwin Steinberg makes a similar suggestion, advocating that NCTE establish an advisory board of "highly competent professional writers to work with college professors of English on composition courses and programs" (150). Others also argued, as well, that teachers of writing should, themselves, be writers. In *Teaching Creative Writing,* Lawrence H. Conrad writes, "The teacher should be himself a writer. He need not have attained fame, or even have published his work. But his knowledge of the problems of the writers, and his sympathy with them, will proceed out of his own continued endeavor to write" (Conrad, qtd. in Myers 116).

27   In 1969, Murray brought this work back to campus when he served as the lead composition instructor in a National Defense Education Act (NDEA)-sponsored summer workshop held at UNH.

1967, for example, Murray had organized each day around a series of lectures and discussions on writerly topics such as pre-writing, writing and rewriting; motivation; assignments; correcting papers; diagnosis and treatment of common writing problems, etc. Nowhere, however, does the itinerary from the workshop indicate that there would be time for participants to actually *write* or consult with Murray, a member of his staff, or other participants *about* writing (NES-DEC Summer Workshop in the Teaching of Writing).[28] This changed in Cambridge, however, where Murray organized his syllabus around not writerly topics or concepts but, rather, the production of two major writing projects: a biography or autobiography on a subject of the students' own choosing and an expository or persuasive piece "concerning a method of teaching writing" (Syllabus and Registration Form) The syllabus for the course shows, further, that Murray established staggered monthly deadlines for students to submit drafts of their work-in-progress throughout the year-long course and designated two hours of each class meeting for individual conferences. In the promotional materials for the seminar, Murray summarizes his approach thus: "The teacher will write so he will experience the problems and solutions of the published writer. At each step he will be shown how this approach may be adapted to the classroom" (Syllabus and Registration Form).

In this way, that year of 1967–68, and with the help of pre-publication chapters of *A Writer Teaches Writing*, Murray walked his students through an early version of what he understood to be a "process" approach to teaching writing, so that they could go back to their own classrooms and do the same with their students. Also Murray began to develop an approach to professional development that would become common in both teacher education programs and Writing Across the Curriculum (WAC) initiatives: ask teachers to write, ask teachers to reflect on their writing, ask teachers to consider the implications of their learning for their teaching of writing.

The most ambitious, albeit unrealized, aspect of Murray and Goodman's collaborations during these years came in the form of a funding request, called Project Write, to launch "a national program to train high school English teachers to become effective writing instructors" (Project Write 13). In their request, Murray and Goodman outline their plans to develop and implement a pilot protocol that would train over 200 New England English teachers in Murray's

---

28 Eventually Murray adjusted his approach at Bowdoin, as he explains in his article "Your Elementary Pupil and the Writer's Cycle of Craft": "At the week-long workshop in the teaching of writing which I conduct for the New England School Development Council at Bowdoin College each summer, I make the teachers write, and when I do they become pupils. They are surprised when they suffer the agonies of their students and even more surprised when I tell them they suffer the agonies of the writer" (9).

writer-based approach to composition pedagogy. These teachers would then implement his method in their classrooms and submit to an assessment protocol that would evaluate the effectiveness of the method with roughly 2,000 students. From the assessment results Murray and Goodman would make adjustments to the approach and launch a more ambitious program to reform the teaching of writing nationwide. Project Write was not just about changing writing pedagogy, however, it was also about changing English. "Composition is but a small part of the English curriculum," Murray and Goodman write in the early pages of their funds request. Citing findings from a joint U.S. Office of Education/ NCTE report they point out that composition is "emphasized only 15.7 percent of the time" in U.S. English classrooms. This, they argue, stems from the fact that teacher education programs do not emphasize composition instruction enough and do not call on actual writers to help shape the training endeavor. In this way, then, Project Write was more than just a proposal to change the way writing is taught in schools, it was also an argument for the reform of the discipline of English, itself (Project Write 10–11).[29]

A Practical Method of Teaching Composition

While their Project Write funding request stands as the most tangible sign of the scope and extent of Murray and Goodman's ambitions, the most concrete outcome of their work together, without a doubt, is *A Writer Teaches Writing: A Practical Method of Teaching Composition*. Now a key work in composition's canon and the most-frequently cited of all of Murray's publications according to Google Scholar, *A Writer Teaches Writing* stands as an artifact of a specific historical moment—in both Murray's career and in the development of composition and rhetoric. Published three years prior to that other canonical early text, Emig's *The Composing Processes of Twelfth Graders*, *A Writer Teaches Writing* predates and anticipates much that was to come in the emergent modern field, beginning with the notion that to learn how to teach writing effectively we must examine the writing processes of writers. In his 1983 review of Emig's book, Ralph F. Voss argues that *The Composing Processes of Twelfth Graders* was "the first significant study of student composing processes, giving impetus to the consciousness of writing as process that prevails in today's composition theory and pedagogy" (278). While Voss' first assertion is certainly true, his second is

---

29   As far as I have been able to tell, after two rounds of trying Murray and Goodman were unsuccessful in identifying a partner to fund the initial stage of their Project Write work, for which they sought $325,000 or roughly $2.5 million in today's dollars (the all-in price for the full project they envisioned was $1.5 million or roughly $12 million in today's dollars). Still, their funding request signals the scope and scale of their plans as well as their intention to reform the teaching of writing and English far beyond NESDEC's regional school network.

surely debatable since Murray, in *A Writer Teaches Writing*, got there first, albeit via a less empirical methodology—autoethnography.[30]

For students of Murray's work, *A Writer Teaches Writing* is many things, a book that was (and still is) unlike almost any other of its kind.[31] It is, first and foremost, an argument for the reform of composition pedagogy and, more broadly, the discipline of English. Second, it's a kind of research report on Murray's writing process,[32] which he takes to be *the* writing process and therefore universally transferable but is really just his interpretation of the process by which he wrote (mostly nonfiction).[33] Third, *A Writer Teaches Writing* is a guide to an inductive, responsive method of teaching writing. It's also a compendium of axioms and advice on writing by famous poets, novelists, and journalists. And it's a plea for student-centered pedagogy. Finally, and most personally, it's an act of retribution against the teachers of Murray's youth. In fact, we might say that when read within the context of Murray's early academic struggles, he had been writing *A Writer Teaches Writing*, or preparing to do so, his entire life.[34] Looking back on his career from the perch of retirement he admits as much himself: "I feel a sense of accomplishment. I am not the great poet and fine novelist of my dreams, but I have published articles, poetry, novels, and a textbook on teaching

---

30   Voss points out, correctly, I believe, that Emig's "science consciousness," something Murray lacked, was largely the cause of her book's successful reception within what was, then, a scientifically aspirational field.

31   It's interesting to note that in the exact year that *A Writer Teaches Writing* was published, in the pages of *College Composition and Communication*, English professor David V. Harrington issued a call for the very sort of book that it was. "It should be said in passing," Harrington writes, "that too many textbook descriptions of how to [write] appear based exclusively upon teaching tradition, hardly at all upon how the writers themselves actually write. There is a need for more introspection, more candidness, even a need for something like a testimonial approach to composition teaching" (7).

32   Writerly self-study was nothing new for Murray. During his years as a freelancer he had taken small steps towards trying to understand his own writing process (his livelihood, after all, depended on it!), keeping daily, weekly, monthly, and yearly word counts of his output and analyzing patterns in his production.

33   To be sure, Murray did not seem to imagine or at least did not much emphasize, at this point in his career, that the process of writing might differ with the genre, audience, or purpose of the task (i.e., the rhetorical situation). As we saw in the last chapter, there was little in Murray's background to give him the language to speak about writing in rhetorical terms. He would later acknowledge that "process" was more complicated than he first understood it to be, claiming that "There is not one process, but many. The process varies with the personality or cognitive style of the writer, the experience of the writer, and the nature of the writing task" (*A Writer Teaches Writing*, 2nd ed. 4).

34   Of the first edition of the book Murray would later write, "To me, *A Writer Teaches Writing* will always be an autobiographical document, the narrative of one writer who attempted to become a teacher of writing in mid-life" (*A Writer Teaches Writing*, rev. 2nd ed. xii).

writing, a satisfying act of revenge against my high school English teachers" (*The Lively Shadow* 47).

To read the first edition of *A Writer Teaches Writing* is to read a writer who is testing new arguments with new audiences and in many cases trying to respectfully push back against the status quo. It is to read a writer who knows he has no right (or interest) to claim membership in the scholarly community of English his colleagues at UNH inhabit, but is just beginning to claim and assert membership in a new, emergent disciplinary community focused on the study of writing and its teaching. It is also to read a writer who is on the cusp of a major professional and life transition and has no idea what's coming. Writing *A Writer Teaches Writing* was a delicate balancing act—Murray wanted to establish credibility and authority with schoolteachers, advance his "practical method of teaching composition," and challenge the existing orthodoxy in English but not in a way that would alienate those, like his UNH colleagues (and former mentors), who were, at the very moment he was drafting the book, deliberating over whether or not he should be awarded promotion and tenure.

My analysis of the first edition of the book suggests that it contains both a curriculum and a hidden curriculum—the former focusing mostly on writing and its teaching, the latter focusing on the relationship between teachers and students. Let's take these one at a time.

Curriculum

If there is one idea around which the official curriculum of *A Writer Teaches Writing* is built it is the proposition that student writers need to experience and understand writing as professionals do, which, according to Murray, is as an activity in which individuals in the process of trying to say something to someone for some reason work to identify and resolve the myriad problems of composing that inevitably arise along writing's way. Professional writers, Murray knew, were, at root, *problem-solvers*. Student writers, however, inexperienced in the problem-solving nature of writing, would not be up to the challenge of real writing (and re-writing, and re-writing *again*), Murray knew, if they were not deeply invested in their work. "The student must spend his time in the lengthy process of discovering and solving his own writing problems," Murray explains in *A Writer Teaches Writing* (105). Students would not, he felt, have the energy to do so if their motivation to write in the first place wasn't grounded in a genuine desire to say something to someone about something important to them.

Through his experience teaching Freshman English at UNH, but also observing high school English teachers in the field, Murray had become acquainted with the kinds of topics English teachers frequently assigned during this era (e.g., in Freshman English: How to Be a Good Friend in a Time of Need, etc.).

All too often Murray found such prompts to be trite, silly, and schoolish. He wanted students to be able to bite into open topics that they, and not their teachers, found meaningful. Further, he felt that English teachers made a mistake when they tried to teach writing by asking students to write about literature. "It is a matter of dogma in many English Departments," he writes, "that students have nothing to say until literature is poured into their heads. We cannot assume that literature is the primary interest of our students—or even that it should be" (106). In a writing class, Murray argued, students should write about multiple different topics in multiple of forms, modes, or genres (the more the better). It mattered that they feel deeply invested in their work. If sufficiently invested they would have a chance to learn what Murray wanted them to learn most—i.e., how to trouble-shoot and problem-solve *while* writing so as to produce an effective working draft.[35]

The idea that English teachers must help students become writing problem-solvers is among the most valuable and interesting curricular elements of *A Writer Teaches Writing*. Who else was talking about writing-as-problem-solving at this time? It wasn't until the mid to late 1970s and 1980s, when scholars like Janet Emig, Nancy Sommers, Sondra Perl, and Linda Flower and John Hayes began to study student writing processes, that we began to understand and develop a language to talk about the problem-solving nature of the work. Murray's ideas in *A Writer Teaches Writing* pre-date and anticipate this way of thinking and they grew out of his concern with an issue that has always been at the heart of our field's work: learning transfer.

Fundamentally, Murray saw his task in *A Writer Teaches Writing* as one of analyzing and dissecting what it was he did when he wrote to identify a transferable process that could be shared with English teachers who could then teach it to students who could then use it to navigate the numerous writing situations they would encounter in and out of school throughout their lives. Given Murray's experience and the state of knowledge in the field at the time, it was a project that made a good deal of sense. "How does the writer write?" Murray asks on the very first page of *A Writer Teaches Writing*. His answer: "We cannot discover how the writer works merely by studying what he has left on the page.

---

35   For the record, while Murray encourages teachers in *A Writer Teaches Writing* to help students find topics about which to write that interest them he's not overly concerned with autobiographical writing (prior to coming to UNH to teach Murray produced very little, if any, such writing himself). The important thing in teaching writing, Murray argued, was not that the student "open a vein" on the page but, rather, that she own the content of her work. So, for example, a student wishing to write an essay about how to ride a motorcycle might also be encouraged "to write a proposal for a new motorcycle law, a letter to the editor answering an editorial against motorcycle riders, a definition of a good motorcyclist, an argument for a new motorcycle design" (134).

We must observe the act of writing itself to expose to our students the process of writing as it is performed by the successful writer" (1). Such a process, Murray felt, would help students develop a transferable process that would serve them well wherever they ended up. After all, as Murray reminds his readers, "We are teaching writers who will write descriptions of automobile accidents and living room suites which are on sale, reports on factory production and laboratory experiments, political speeches and the minutes of League of Women Voters meetings, love letters and business letters" (154). As a professional writer from beyond academia, Murray understood, in ways that most English teachers and professors probably did or could not, where students were headed as writers after high school or college and he wanted to try to help prepare them for these myriad writerly futures.

Of what did Murray's early teaching-for-transfer approach consist? In *A Writer Teaches Writing*'s first chapter Murray outlines what he understands to be the seven core activities of writing, which he then develops and elaborates on in greater detail in following chapters. The writer, he argues, discovers a subject, senses an audience, searches for specifics, creates a design, writes, develops a critical eye, and rewrites. While the genre, for Murray circa 1968, may change, the process doesn't. "If you can write a sonnet you can write an advertisement," he posits, "if you can produce a novel you can produce a company report" (231). Well, not really, as we now know. In the fifty-plus years since *A Writer Teaches Writing* was published, our knowledge of what happens when writers write (and of how transfer happens . . . or fails to) has broadened, deepened, and expanded exponentially. We should not blame earlier theorists and scholars, however, for not knowing what we know now. *A Writer Teaches Writing* is a product of its time—a time, in this case, when few, if any, empirical studies of writers writing had been published, when the term rhetorical situation had only recently been coined, and when the notion of *genre* in the English classroom referred to literary forms (poems, novels, short stories, and plays). In light of all this, Murray's investigations into his own writing process circa 1966 or so as he worked to draft *A Writer Teaches Writing* can be likened to an amateur archeologist stumbling into an undiscovered cave with a flashlight. The report on the process of discovery might not hold up to later scrutiny, and the conclusions drawn from the investigations will, later, be reconsidered and revised, but you must still give credit to the early investigators for their attempts to explore and understand what was previously not understood.

Murray's interest in and advocacy for explicit reflection in *A Writer Teaches Writing*, too, counts as a significant element of his curriculum worth highlighting. "It's helpful," he urges his readers, "to have students write about writing. . . . When you write about writing you have to focus on how to write as well as what to write, and the combination can be very helpful for the student" [170]). From the perspective of history, then, what I see as the core of *A Writer Teaches Writing*'s curriculum—a vision of writing as problem-solving, a focus on transfer, and an early articulation of the value of metacognition to the writing process, are not small contributions to the knowledge of our field. Murray's concern for these issues pre-dates and sets the stage for much of what was to come in composition scholarship in the years to follow.

Hidden Curriculum

The hidden curriculum of *A Writer Teaches Writing*, perhaps harder to discern, is woven throughout the book and is principally about the relationship between teachers and students. It's in the hidden curriculum that we find Murray's arguments for a student-centered approach to teaching and learning that forwards the causes of empowerment, social justice, and diversity. Mina Shaughnessy is largely credited with embodying this vision during the field's earliest days but a decade before Shaughnessy and a half dozen years before NCTE's "Students' Right to Their Own Language" Murray was working, in his own way, to inscribe in composition and rhetoric the deeply humane pedagogical vision that has long been an essential characteristic of our discipline.

While the immediate exigence for *A Writer Teaches Writing* was, as we have seen, rooted in Murray's work with NESDEC, a deeper exigence can be traced to his own debilitating early years of schooling, to his literacy narrative. Deep into the book one finds evidence of the way in which Murray's own personal story influenced and informed the book's writing:

> This may be the time to mention that I quit high school each year and did not graduate. My parents were told that I did not belong in school. When I see how quickly and how permanently many of our students are evaluated, I cannot forget the years when I was told I was stupid, year after year, and I believed it. (160)

As we saw in the last chapter, Murray felt himself to be an outsider in school. He considered himself a casualty of what he dubbed the "not-so-good-old-days" of public education and of a Depression-era school system that he felt failed to account for the diversity and difference—in knowing, in thinking, in learning, in communicating—that he brought to the classroom. In sum, the personal exigence for *A Writer Teaches Writing* was Murray's lifelong belief that as a child he was a victim of educational injustice. His books and articles, starting with *A Writer Teaches Writing*, were efforts to set things right.

Given Murray's painful, silencing experiences in school growing up it's perhaps not surprising that the word *listen* plays such a prominent role in the hidden curriculum of *A Writer Teaches Writing*. In the second chapter, Murray lists "He Listens" as the first of the seven skills that an effective teacher must learn and practice. Inhabiting what might be called *a listening stance* was an essential element of an empowering pedagogy for Murray. Teachers must learn to become effective listeners, he believed, so that they could see, understand, and, most importantly, accept each student as he/she was. "When you talk to those teachers who motivate students," Murray writes, "you begin to see [that] they are all interested in knowing the student as an individual. They listen to the student and the student knows it" (151). To be fair, this was a tall ask for high school English teachers facing 100–150 students a day, but Murray asked anyway because he felt it was what students, and especially those students who didn't easily fit into an inflexible educational system, were due.

Enacting a listening stance, as Murray goes on to explain in *A Writer Teaches Writing*, does not mean the teacher must "accept the student's view of the world if it is irrational, illogical and expressed in an illiterate manner." It does mean that the teacher must "listen to what he [*sic*] has to say," not what he or she "wish[es] he would say but what he has to say. . . . Each student is at a different point" (16). This idea of *difference*, of each student being "at a different point," is another important element that Murray develops and elaborates throughout *A Writer Teaches Writing*, a key aspect of the hidden curriculum, largely under the umbrella of acknowledging, accepting, and celebrating intellectual diversity (not a term Murray used). "Each student," he writes, "is working at his own pace and his relationship to other students in the class is relatively unimportant" (16). Education, for Murray, wasn't a race to the top, nor should it be. It was a highly individualized developmental process to which teachers needed to adapt themselves.

If, for Murray, the teacher must be a person who listens, then the classroom must be a different kind of place than what it usually is. Murray advocates for nothing short of a reversal of roles between teachers and students. "The relation of the teacher to his students," he writes, "should be the opposite of the relationship one would expect to find." Usually, he continues, "it is the teacher who knows, the student who learns. Here it is the student who knows, or should, and the teacher who learns, or tries to" (17). In this way, in Murray's reformed classroom, the student reads and writes about the things he or she knows or wishes to know and the teacher listens (on the page, in the classroom, in the conference) and responds. In this way, teaching becomes a process in which teachers do research on students and their learning in order to discern how to teach them effectively. Murray never uses the term *student-centered* in *A Writer Teaches Writing*, but as all of this suggests, it's very much what he had in mind (throughout his career, Murray preferred to think of his approach as *responsive* or *conference* teaching). In this way Murray, writing circa 1966 or so, very much anticipated one of the key tenets of what would become the writing process movement: students, their writing, and their processes of learning to write constitute the "content" of a writing class.

As a savvy rhetorician anticipating push-back from his elders, Murray cues into the historical moment of cultural upheaval in *A Writer Teaches Writing* to argue, finally, that a responsive, listening-based pedagogy is necessitated by the times. In an era of "mass society, mass communications and mass mind," Murray writes, there can be no more important task for a teacher than to empower his or her students to develop a sense of voice by listening to them (17). Further, he argues, tapping into the emergent social justice ethos of the era, "What we should do is attempt to give everyone freedom of opportunity [to learn] regardless of his background, his race, his religion, or the limitations with which he came to the classroom" (154). In offering all students the opportunity to write (which is to say to speak, to be heard, to be listened to), Murray invites his readers to situate the day-to-day work of teaching and learning in a truly humanistic vision. "A man's drive to tell another what he knows about life—to relate, to sympathize, to incite, to educate, to entertain, to persuade—starts with a baby's first cry and lasts until an old man's final words," Murray writes. "The effective writing teacher mobilizes this force simply by allowing his students to speak" (151). Within this vision, writing, finally, is an act in which "one single human being [is] speaking to another single human being" (17). Humans speaking to humans—this gets at the heart of the hidden curriculum of *A Writer Teaches Writing*.

CONCLUSION

In this chapter, I have tried to show how Donald Murray's early teaching at UNH and his collaborations with NESDEC were instrumental in drawing him into a new career path as a reformer of composition pedagogy, the discipline of English, and the traditional processes of schooling. NESDEC offered Murray the opportunity to take ideas and theories he had begun to develop through his work with pre-service teachers at UNH and operationalize them via numerous professional development initiatives and, ultimately, a proposal for an ambitious (ultimately unfunded) grant-seeking effort (i.e., Project Write). It also provided him with resources to write his first book about writing, *A Writer Teaches Writing*. In short, with NESDEC's help Murray went from being a writer and aspiring novelist to something he had never planned to become—a writer teaching writing—and teaching *teachers* of writing, as well.

What makes Murray's work during these years notable is the extent to which it was all so unexpected and unanticipated. As we have seen, Murray's intention when he transitioned to UNH was to find more time to write fiction, but in a 1968 memo to new English Department chair Jack Richardson, he outlines his "changing role" at the university without even mentioning those plans. Of his primary role, the one he was hired to play as head of journalism, Murray notes that his work in this regard has "not expanded." Of his newfound role as a "teacher of teachers of composition," Murray explains, his work in this area is "expanding, especially on [the] graduate level." It is, he writes, his "greatest interest, now and for a few years" (Letter to Jack Richardson).

Murray's teaching schedule, publication trajectory, and growing calendar of speaking engagements all confirm that he was, by the mid to late 1960s, committing himself to an entirely new professional path. While he continued to teach journalism and non-fiction throughout his career his teaching schedule at UNH, beginning in the early 1970s, regularly included graduate seminars in composition theory and pedagogy (he taught UNH's first such course, Seminar in Teaching Writing, in the fall of 1972). His publishing agenda underwent a complete overhaul at this time, as well. Each year from 1963 to 1967 the number of articles Murray placed in periodicals like those in which he had published prior to transitioning to UNH declined. In 1968, for the first time, he placed no such pieces but, instead, presented two papers at professional conferences for English teachers, published his first articles on writing and pedagogy in small academic journals, and published *A Writer Teaches Writing*. With regular invitations to speak about writing and teaching at schools in New Hampshire and beyond and commitments to serve on various state education boards and committees, including the New Hampshire Council for Teacher Education, Murray's professional transformation was, by the early 1970s, mostly complete.

As we learn from his personal correspondence from this time, however, Murray's new work with teachers was not always easy or happy. It was even something he sometimes tried to escape. In the winter of 1970, for example, in a letter in which he urged NESDEC to abandon its plans for a fourth summer workshop at Bowdoin, Murray writes, "I am too impatient to work well with teachers in in-service programs, and prefer to concentrate on developing written materials which other people may choose to use in such programs" (Letter to Robert S. Ireland). In a lengthy letter written about this same time to Dick Goodman, Murray is more expansive on the nature of his struggles. "I can not seem to make education central to my life," he writes. Further, he admits, while he has enjoyed working with teachers, he would like to make such work "less a part of [his] life." In a particularly damning and, frankly, surprising passage, he expresses the full extent of his frustrations, claiming that it's actually teachers who are the main thing that is "wrong with education":

> We can do a lot to improve the education of teachers, and I
> think we have. . . . But we can't seem to do much about the
> kind of people we get in education. . . . The more I work
> with teachers the more I am convinced that the majority
> of them are frightened of their students, terrified of their
> administrators, resentful and afraid of parents and taxpayers,
> scared of each other, and apprehensive that there may be some
> change in the subject matter they teach. This is not a matter
> of education, for the teacher can raise the sophistication level
> of his jargon, add graduate degrees, and still be an essentially
> frightened and passive individual. (Letter to Dr. Richard
> Goodman)

It's an uncomfortable indictment from a man who, elsewhere, was a champion of teachers but apparently still carried with him the legacy of his childhood struggles. Murray acknowledges as much himself, confessing that his problem with teachers is just as likely to stem from his own failures, as he is, he admits, too often "arrogant, impatient, and idealistic." Nonetheless, he explains, in the years ahead he will "remove [him]self more and more from working directly in education outside of [his] own university courses" (Letter to Dr. Richard Goodman).

Of course, that's not what happened. Murray's work with teachers was far from over in the early 1970s. It was, in fact, just beginning and while his audience evolved over the years, with his writing and talks increasingly addressing college-level writing instructors and researchers, Murray never stopped speaking to K–12 teachers. As composition and rhetoric evolved as a field during the 1970s and 1980s, Murray did, too, though. He was able to do so, in large part, and as we will see in the next chapter, because of his extensive work on campus at UNH, as he worked to build on and extend the legacy of Dr. Carroll Towle to create a new culture and community around the study of writing and its teaching.

CHAPTER 3.

TRANSFORMING A LOCAL WRITING TRADITION, 1971–1977

The core of the present UNH freshmen English program was established when Don Murray directed the program in the early seventies

– Gary Lindberg, New Methods in College Writing Programs

The late 1960s and the early 1970s must be seen as a time of fundamental change in the teaching of writing. It was during this period that Donald Murray purified Freshman English at the University of New Hampshire.

– Thomas Newkirk, "Locating Freshman English"

Today we swim in an ocean of composition theory but when I taught my first Freshman English class thirty years ago I was offered no theories and, in fact, when I asked my department head told me, "One doesn't talk about teaching methods. That's a matter of academic freedom."

– Donald Murray, "Tricks of the Trade"

In the third epigraph, above, Donald Murray recalls a time during his early years on the faculty at UNH when English professors might have spoken about the *what* of teaching writing but not so much its *how*. Within the liberal culture orthodoxy that reigned in the Department during the period when Murray was a student and, briefly, when he returned as a faculty member, the key pedagogical imperative was *exposure*—exposure to literary texts and other key elements of the western cultural tradition. *How* one exposed one's students to these things was, by Murray's testimony, apparently one's own business and not something which necessitated discussion. In the minds of some faculty members of the department's second epoch, teaching's how, at least as Murray recalls it, was off-limits, a matter of "academic freedom."

Over the course of his first years on campus and then throughout his career at UNH, Donald Murray worked to oppose this don't-ask-don't-tell approach to teaching and learning. With the help of numerous others, Murray worked to revise and transform the teaching of writing and to make discussions of composition pedagogy, in Freshman English and beyond, a normal aspect of department (and campus) life. His efforts to, as Newkirk puts it in the second epigraph above, "purify" Freshman English consisted, eventually, of removing all of the normal trappings of a college composition class, i.e., assignments, readings, grades, conceptual material, and even, as we will see, class meetings themselves. In this way, Murray helped establish at UNH during the early heady years of the writing process movement an approach to composition pedagogy grounded in the experiential knowledge of the professional writer as he understood the term. This method, which gained the university a national reputation in composition teaching, came to serve as a model for countless others in the emergent field (see, for example, Moran). At UNH it was an approach which, as we learn from Gary Lindberg, a literary scholar who directed Freshman English in the 1980s, would guide the teaching of composition at the university for many years to come.

In this chapter, I offer, first, an exploration of the conditions on campus at UNH that made Murray's reforms possible before moving on to describe the processes by which he and his collaborators worked to create a new kind of college composition class at the university. If the story of the last chapter was one of Murray's partnerships with school teachers and, in particular, NESDEC, to reform the teaching of writing in secondary and primary schools, the story of this one centers on his collaborations with colleagues at UNH to reform the teaching of college composition. On the one hand, it's a story about how Murray and others worked to integrate elements of the university's long-standing extracurricular writing tradition into the curriculum. On the other hand, it's a story about how Murray and others went beyond that tradition to challenge the existent approach to the teaching of composition that arose at the university during the English Department's second epoch. Cumulatively, it's a story about how Murray and others built on the writing culture that Dr. Carroll Towle established at UNH during the war years, preserving the institution's reputation as a "writer's university" while extending it to become a writing *teacher's* university, all while laying the groundwork for it to later become a writing *researcher's* university, as well.

TIMES A' CHANGIN'

As we learned in an earlier chapter, when Donald Murray enrolled at UNH in the late 1940s he joined, as he put it, a "community of men and women who were writers, or who dreamed of being writers." As we observed with Tirabassi, however, this community was largely an extracurricular affair. The teaching of writing within the formal curriculum at UNH during the pre- and post-war years, and especially within general education, was rooted in a conservative curricular vision that was typical of the era (see Masters).

Beginning in the 1960s, however, change began to come to the UNH English Department, change which impacted all aspects of its work, including its methods for teaching composition. First, there was the natural attrition of the faculty.

Epoch Two professors who had arrived in the 1930s and shaped the vision and direction of the department throughout the middle years of the twentieth century were, by the early to mid 1960s, passing the torch to a new generation of faculty members. Dr. Bingham, perhaps the strongest advocate of the liberal culture project, stepped down as department chairman in 1966 and retired a year or so later. With his departure came the closing of the department's second epoch and a gradual relaxing of its commitment to the liberal culture ethos. One tangible sign of this change came in 1968, when the department revised the English major to once again allow students to take writing and other non-literary courses towards completion of the major. English became, then, once again, no longer synonymous with just the study of literature and liberal culture.

A second important change that took place around this time occurred in 1962 when the novelist Thomas Williams—an alum, like Murray, of the UNH English Department—was promoted from an instructor position onto the tenure track, becoming, in the process, the first creative writer to achieve such status. Williams' advancement and the subsequent hiring of a stable of additional writers into tenure-line positions in the years that followed was notable in a department that had long prioritized literature and those who could teach it over writing.[36] From a faculty perspective, then, the UNH English Department became, in the 1960s, a place that was hospitable to, even welcoming of, writers, and this inevitably changed the department's orientation towards its work and its sense of identity.[37] By 1973, when future Pulitzer Prize-winner and U.S. poet-Laureate Charles Simic arrived, fully one-quarter of the tenured or tenure-line faculty members in the department were writers. These men, "the writers," as they came to be called, transformed the department during the dawning years of its third epoch.

A third significant factor impacting Murray's work at UNH during 1960s and beyond was one that affected the university as a whole, but contained specific implications for English. With the arrival of the baby-boomers on campus

---

36   In 1967 the novelists Mark Smith and Theodore Weesner joined Williams and John Yount, who was hired in 1963, on the tenure track. Alongside these full-time professional novelists was a growing cohort of part-time/adjunct instructors and graduate students who were writers or aspiring writers, including, at one time or another, John Irving, Ursula Hegi, Alice McDermott, and Russell Banks.

37   Viewed within the context of the growth of creative writing in higher education at this time, these changes make sense. As Myers has argued, the post-war period was one when universities came "to provide institutional sanctuary for the arts, including literature" (148). From the 1940s through the 1970s, and especially paralleling the 1960s boom in post-secondary enrollments, new undergraduate and graduate programs in creative writing were established with rapidity at U.S. colleges and universities (Myers 146–49). Thus, the story of the growth of writing, and creative writing, in particular, at UNH can be understood as a local story but can also be placed within a larger narrative about disciplinary change in English at this time.

in the early 1960s, UNH's student body began to grow, nearly doubling by the end of the decade. This increase in students forced change in virtually every aspect of university life.[38] In the English Department, this meant a shift towards a greater reliance on contingent faculty members to teach the growing number of sections of Freshman English. During the 1964–65 academic year, just seven part-timers are listed among department personnel (*Bulletin* 1964–65 167). By 1966, that number doubled (*Bulletin* 1966–67, 181). It peaked in 1970, when seventeen "Instructors" were listed *(Bulletin* 1969–1970 171–72).[39] As notable, in 1966 a non-tenure track faculty member was appointed to direct Freshman English for the first time (*Bulletin* 1966–67, 181). The incredible increase in the number of students and the attendant shift and expansion this forced in department personnel within English created a new hierarchy within the English Department , creating two distinct groups or classes, the "junior" and "senior" faculty. This division would soon create problems, particularly in the teaching of Freshman English, as junior faculty members grew frustrated implementing what they perceived to be an outdated curriculum that they were hired to teach but had little voice in creating.

Fourth, and finally, it's important to note that UNH, as an institution, underwent considerable transition and reinvention during the latter post-war years. As UNH historian James has shown, from the late 1940s on the university worked to shift its institutional profile in the direction of doctoral education and faculty scholarship. In keeping with this change, the English Department commenced work on a doctoral program in the early 1960s, the first in the College of Liberal Arts, (it would take the entire decade to bring the program to fruition).[40] As English faculty were given a reduction in their teaching loads to make time for more scholarly endeavors, as these same faculty members shifted their intellectual energies away from undergraduate and towards graduate education, and as new faculty members with hefty research credentials and impressive publication records were hired to bolster the department's scholarly credibility, the UNH English Department became a different kind of place in the late sixties

---

38   According to UNH historian Marion James, immediate post-war enrollment at UNH stood at around 5,800 students. By the mid to late 1960s, the student population had grown to over 10,000 (9).

39   With a new doctoral program coming online around 1970 or so, pressure to hire part-timers eventually abated as Freshman English was increasingly taught by graduate teaching assistants. In this way, the UNH English Department's labor practices caught up to what had been happening elsewhere in college English for decades.

40   While the exigence for the creation of this program was entirely local, it's worth noting that graduate programs in English were on the rise across the US in the 1960s. According to Geckle, the number of graduate programs in institutions of higher education increased by over 50% during the decade (43).

and early seventies. No longer a sleepy backwater in which most English faculty were committed to undergraduate and general education and almost all ascribed to a genteel liberal culture tradition, the department became, in the 1960s and beyond, a place that was concerned less with the preservation of knowledge and more with its creation.

In sum, numerous factors, some local to UNH, others generalized across higher education, coalesced in the 1960s and 1970s to create a transitional institutional environment in which Donald Murray and others could make the case for curricular and pedagogical reform. The times were a' changin', as the old lyric goes, and while Murray, 39 when he transitioned to college teaching, was not *of* the times, he tapped *into* them as he worked to advance arguments for educational and disciplinary change.

IN FRESHMAN ENGLISH

According to Thomas Masters "Arnoldian ideology" permeated and infused college composition instruction in U.S. higher education during the pre- and post-war years (106). Masters found that part of the teaching of composition at this time was "the production of texts that would demonstrate the degree to which students had learned standards of correctness and rudiments of academic style" and part of instruction focused on "the reading and discussion of literature" (136). So it was at UNH, where the catalogue description for Freshman English from 1946 through the late 1960s described the class as "The training of students to write correctly and with force and to read with appreciation and discernment the chief types of literature" (*Bulletin* 1946 211). Further, Tirabassi's detailed analysis of Freshman English in the 1940s confirms that it was a standard affair for its time, with a first semester course centered on expository writing and a second semester class focused on literature. Both English 1 (later 401) and 2 (later 402) were organized around a tightly scripted schedule of readings and assignments from which faculty members were not to deviate. In English 1/401, students learned about various concepts of expository writing, i.e., coherence, unity, clarity, but also style, paragraphing, and sentence structure, and they read essays that served as models of exemplary composition, examples to illustrate writing concepts, and tools to instill the liberal culture subjectivity. They wrote ten themes in English 1/401, half of which were composed in class.[41] In English

---

41   Students were allowed to choose the content of their themes but seem to have frequently run with bland topics, as suggested by the banal and milquetoast titles they gave their pieces, e.g., "Campus vs. Home," "Leaving Cherished People and Things Behind," "The Jump from High School to College." As sample papers from the era illustrate, some instructors line-edited students' work mercilessly and demanded they edit and resubmit to receive credit. So deter-

2/402 students read and wrote about literary texts selected for their significance to the western cultural tradition and wrote a research paper. Archival documents from the period suggest that the discussions of the Freshman English Planning Committee tended to center on such workaday topics as whether to introduce a new reader into English 1/401 or how many themes to have students write in class as opposed to out of class. Rarely, it seems, was the overarching purpose of or rationale for the course considered or questioned. As a result, little changed in the teaching of Freshman English at UNH from the mid 1940s through the early to mid 1960s, and given the long reign of department chair Bingham, who frequently served on the Freshman English planning committee, we should not be surprised at the continuity and consistency of the program.

From the moment he arrived on campus in 1963, Donald Murray articulated reservations about the teaching of Freshman English. In his report to Dr. Bingham on his first semester in the classroom he writes,

> Since I have been appointed to the committee planning this
> course for next year, I will express my questions about the
> course through the committee. In general I feel it is important
> that the students be given an opportunity to write. . . . The
> majority of the students have not had to write in high school,
> and I feel that I must in Engl. 1 prepare them for the writing
> they will have to do in college. (Report on First Semester)

Rather than assign the ten required themes in his section, Murray goes on to explain that he assigned seventeen. A few students, he reports, "developed some understanding" of the principles of composition. Several months later, in his report on the second semester, Murray returns to this issue of the quantity of writing assignments in Freshman English: "I believe that writing in itself teaches writing," he explains, "and the students desperately need more writing assignments." Further, he argues, students must "rewrite to learn anything about the craft of writing." He will, he reports, conduct a small experiment when teaching English 1 again in the fall, whereby he will require students to rewrite or revise about a third of their pieces. "I want [my students] to experience the craft of writing and rewriting," Murray explains in a passage that foreshadows arguments he would go on to develop in the years to come. "I want them to approximate whenever possible the job of the professional writer" (Murray, Report on Second Semester).

---

mined, in fact, was the Freshman English faculty of this era to do right by its colleagues across campus in its commitment to root error out of student writing, a policy was created which allowed any UNH faculty member to remand back to Freshman English at any time any student whose writing was found wanting.

Despite Murray's growing reputation off campus as a kind of writing guru, he was passed over twice as director of Freshman English during his early years on the faculty. Perhaps he wasn't passed over, though. Perhaps he was sufficiently busy writing and field-testing *A Writer Teaches Writing* and seeking grant funding for a national program to reform the teaching of composition in K–12 education that it never occurred to him that he might *want* to become director of Freshman English.[42] We'll never know for sure. In any event, Murray moved on from teaching Freshman English and serving on its planning committee in 1966, but penned, on his way out the door, an exhaustive five-page single-spaced memo to the committee outlining his concerns about the course and its teaching (he had secured tenure and promotion earlier that year).[43] As he makes clear in his memo, Murray found the aims and purposes of Freshman English at UNH to be almost totally incomprehensible. If the course was supposed to be a general education class, he asks, why did some faculty treat it like "an introduction to the humanities"? If, in the eyes of many in the department, it was deemed a "remedial course," why were there honors sections? And if faculty were not, in English 402, teaching a course that was intended to serve as an introduction to literary studies, as some in the department apparently claimed, what *were* they teaching? In the closing of his memo Murray underscores his over-arching confusion about the aims and purposes of Freshman English at UNH: "The important thing is to have a clear understanding of exactly what it is we want to teach," he writes (Freshman English). In this way, he echoes Albert Kitzhaber who, in his report on a nationwide study of Freshman English conducted around this same time, concluded, "There are quite as many things wrong with freshman English in college as with English in high school," many of which "arise from a vast uncertainty about aims, about content, about methods" (99). Murray seems to have found, in the local setting of UNH, an example of what Kitzhaber observed nationally. He was not, however, bent on trying to reform Freshman English at this time. He taught ENGL 402 for the last time in the spring of 1966, stepped down from the planning committee, and moved on.

---

42   Or, perhaps, as Murray indicates in a letter to a friend in the months just before he was eventually appointed director, in 1971, he "did not wish to become involved" in Freshman English, preferring, instead, to teach "courses which in no way impinge upon [his] colleagues'" areas of expertise. (Dear John)

43   Beyond his colleagues at UNH, Murray began to share his concerns about the teaching of college composition more broadly during these years, as well, publishing his first articles in journals aimed at post-secondary audiences, i.e., "Finding Your Own Voice: Teaching Composition in an age of Dissent," (*CCC*, 1969), "The Interior View: One Writer's Philosophy of Composition" (*CCC*, 1970), and "Perhaps the Professor Should Cut Class" (*College English*, 1973), co-written with UNH colleague Lester Fisher.

BIRTH OF AN UNWRITING CLASS

Between 1966 and 1971, as the UNH English Department launched a new doctoral program in literature and largely abandoned it to the "junior faculty," Murray got to work trying to imagine, on his own terms, a new kind of college composition course whose purpose was neither the remediation of students' writerly deficiencies nor their enculturation into the liberal culture ethos. The course he built served as a blueprint for a redesigned class once Murray took over as director in 1971. The seeds for this new course, English 501, Expository Writing, were planted in 1966 when Murray drafted a memo to new department chair Jack Richardson with a proposal for a sophomore-level advanced writing elective. The proposal stemmed from the fact that demand for Murray's services among UNH students was already exceeding supply. His experience trying to accommodate all who wanted a seat in Expository Writing had, he writes, "dramatized the need for a basic course in expository writing, which will serve the university in giving students something beyond 401 without getting them involved in the writing of fiction and poetry" (Guidelines).[44] One could have argued that English 401 *was* a "basic course in expository writing" that was intended to "serve the university" and ask why, if Freshman English was doing its job, students should need or want more, but Murray left such questions unasked.

In follow-up correspondence with Richardson from 1967, Murray goes into significant detail regarding his vision for English 501, the curriculum of which served as a distinct contrast with and departure from that of Freshman English. If Freshman English was a typical college writing course for its era, English 501 would be an atypical college *un*writing course. First, there would be no grades in English 501, or, at least, evaluation would be deferred until the end of the term. This, Murray insisted, would "reduce the pressure of writing for a grade" which, he felt, undermined the entire enterprise of learning to write effectively.[45] Second, in ENGL 501, there would no longer be the traditional "content" of a writing course typical at UNH, i.e., didactic lectures on abstract concerns such as style, organization, paragraphing, etc. The "content" would, instead, be "the student's own writing." Third, there would be little, if any, reading in English 501 and that which was assigned would consist mostly of "articles on writing by writers," so that students would "learn to see the problem of writing from the writer's point of view." Fourth, there would be no assignments in English 501, at least not in

---

44   As we saw in the last chapter, initially, expository writing to be taken by pre-service teachers. It was, however, once Murray began to teach the class, increasingly popular among regular English majors who were interested in writing, as well.

45   Murray's work in this regard anticipates alternative approaches to assessment that would follow in future years, e.g., grading contracts and, more recently, labor-based grading.

the traditional sense. Rather, each week students would write something new or revise something they had already written and instructors would provide feedback, ideally in conference, on work-in-progress. In ENGL 501, then, students would learn the skills of the practicing writer as Murray understood them by participating in a work cycle that looked less like that practiced by the typical college student and more like that of the professional writer (ENGLISH 501).

Murray first taught English 501 in the fall 1966. By spring 1971 six sections of the class were being offered each semester.[46] This created an opportunity for him to enlist others in the endeavor and to begin to think of himself in new ways—as a writing program administrator and a writing researcher. As to the former, Murray got to work in early 1971 to codify procedures for teaching in what was quickly becoming known as the English 501 "program." In a course overview document for students he describes the class as an opportunity "to learn to write by facing and solving the basic problems of the writer" and then answers three pages of imagined questions about the class (e.g., "You mean a student can write about anything?" *Yes.* "Will we have conferences with the instructors?" *Yes.* And so on.). In a separate document aimed at the English 501 staff, Murray outlines purposes and procedures for the course and identifies himself as the administrator. "Professor Murray will direct the course," he writes, "and he will have final say over the staff, approve the methods used to teach the course, participate in the planning and scheduling, and run a series of meetings for the staff." Having moved on from Freshman English, albeit temporarily, Murray had, it seems, created a new composition program all of his own making (English 501).

Beyond this new work as a writing program administrator, Murray's experience with English 501 also gave him the chance to become a kind of writing researcher. In a department where research and scholarship were the currency of the day and at a time when Murray was increasingly advising and teaching graduate students, his work in English 501 gave him the opportunity to begin to imagine himself as more than just a writer *teaching* writing but also, now, a writer *studying* writing and its teaching. In 1970, he teamed up with a young instructor, Lester Fisher, to write a grant to UNH's Council for Educational Innovation to address the "problem" of too-great demand for English 501. In their proposal, Murray and Fisher lay out an approach to composition pedagogy that challenges not just the idea that the class meeting is the essential element of a college course but that the semester is the essential unit of the college calendar.

---

46   Demand for English 501 continued to grow in the years to come, to the point that, by the late 1970s and early 1980s, when Murray again directed the course, the English Department offered about 40 sections per year. With an administrator and a staff that overlapped with that of Freshman English, English 501 came to function as a kind of secondary writing program within the department during these years. (Faculty Annual Review 1980–81).

They describe an experimental design for English 501 which emphasizes "the important parts of [a writing class]—student writing and instructor responding" and "eliminate[es] the traditional but possibly unnecessary class meetings."[47] In their experimental sections, they propose, rather than enroll twenty students, hold class two or three times a week, and conduct bi-weekly student conferences, they will enroll thirty students, eliminate class meetings entirely, and hold conferences with every student every week (Memo to Council for Educational Innovation). In addition to eliminating class meetings, Murray and Fisher describe an administrative structure for their experiment that will transform the traditional timeline of the semester. They propose that with a constant waitlist of students trying to get a seat in English 501, those who do not get a spot initially will be allowed to add the course later in a kind of rolling fashion, as seats come open. And seats will come open, they explain, because some students will be allowed to complete the course in an accelerated fashion while others, who fail to do the work, will be dropped. In this way, students who are unable to get a spot in English 501 at the start of the term will have the opportunity to register for, enroll in, and complete the course at various moments throughout the semester and the academic year (Memo to Council for Educational Innovation).

The Council approved Murray and Fisher's proposal and the two taught their experimental sections that fall of 1970. In November, they traveled to NCTE to share their findings, and a year or so later they brought the process to scholarly fruition by publishing an article about their work in *College English*, "Perhaps the Professor Should Cut Class." In the piece Murray and Fisher share what they learned from their "experiment." Here are a few highlights:

1. *On the importance of not over-teaching*: "It is not [the teacher's] responsibility to correct a paper line by line, to rewrite it until it is his own writing" (172).
2. *On spoken response being more effective than written*: "In conference the student and the teacher may read each other's voice and face until they are sure they understand each other" (172).
3. *On teaching by conference being pedagogically efficacious*: "[A]ll the predictors of success in composition—test scores, academic record, social-economic background, maturity—simply d[o] not predict individual performance" (171).

---

47   In a letter to an administrator a few years later, detailing his responsibilities at the college, Murray offers a memorable analogy to try to convey why he deems the writing conference to be the essential activity of a composition class. "I teach little in class, a great deal in conference," he explains. "That's the way it has to be. I don't teach my students in a bunch any more than my doctor can give everyone in the waiting room the same pill" (Letter to Dr. David W. Ellis)

In the end, Murray and Fisher acknowledge that while their experimental approach likely didn't succeed with all students "almost all of those who made a genuine commitment to their work [regardless of background] improved demonstrably" (173). Of course, we should take Murray and Fisher's optimistic conclusions with a grain of salt, but we should also acknowledge the boldness of their experiment and their efforts to develop an innovative solution to a complex institutional problem while simultaneously pushing composition pedagogy in more student-centered directions.[48]

Murray's work developing, administering, and then researching and writing about English 501 gave him important experiences to draw on when the opportunity to become Freshman English director presented itself in the late spring of 1971. No longer a writing "guru" with a following of mostly K–12 teachers, Murray was, by the time he took over as Freshman English director, a curriculum designer, a (lightly) seasoned writing program administrator, a writing researcher of sorts, and a published author of writing aimed at a national audience of college English professors. From 1968 on he was increasingly invited to give talks and lectures on writing and pedagogy at colleges and universities in and around New England and the country. In 1970, he secured a contract with the publisher of *A Writer Teaches Writing*, Houghton Mifflin, to produce a college level textbook ("Faculty Annual Report, 1970–71").[49] In 1972, he joined forces with Professor Tom Carnicelli to teach in a federal grant-funded initiative to train junior college faculty in composition pedagogy. Also in 1972, he was invited to apply for the position of editor at *College Composition and Communication* (he declined) (Letter to Robert F. Hogan). All these developments signal Murray's growing stature within the community of college writing teachers and scholars at this time.

REFORMING FRESHMAN ENGLISH

In the second epigraph at the start of this chapter, Thomas Newkirk makes the claim that during a time of "fundamental change in the teaching of writing" Donald Murray "purified Freshman English at the University of New Hampshire" (3). To say that Murray purified Freshman English is to suggest that it was,

---

48   There is evidence that the innovative administrative structure of the experiment, with rolling admissions and completions, was not entirely a success. In Murray's annual report for the year 1970–71 he writes, "We taught English 501 without class meetings and entirely by individual conference. That was the part of the experiment that was most effective" ("Faculty Annual Report, 1970–71")

49   Murray wouldn't publish a textbook aimed at a college audience for another dozen or more years. In 1984 he published the first edition of *Write to Learn*. The following year, 1985, he brought out his first college reader, *Read to Write*.

in its pre-Murray state, somehow corrupted, but, really, as we have seen, it was mostly just *typical*, a product of its time. To be sure, once ensconced in the position of Freshman English director, Murray did implement reforms to the course, and he drew, to a significant extent, on his experience with English 501 to do so. Under his leadership, weekly meetings were created for the Freshman English staff, conferences became a more central element of instruction, literature (and reading, in general) was all but banished from the curriculum, and instructors were encouraged to find ways to disentangle formative from summative assessment. In short, under Murray's direction English 401 came to look a lot like English 501, and this would be the case for many years to come.

Surprisingly, very few documents from Murray's years as Freshman English director survive in his archive to document the years he worked as the course's administrator. It's an unusual archival omission from a man who wrote copiously about most aspects of his work in his annual musings and saved virtually everything. "I hope I have created a productive diversity in the approaches to Freshman English, and was able to support individual teachers as they attempted to solve their own problems in the teaching of [the course]," he writes in his 1971–72 annual review, the only time he mentions his work as director in any detail in his reviews ("Faculty Annual Report, 1971–72").[50]

An accounting of Murray's weekly hours at the university in his 1972–73 annual review suggests that if he had little to say about directing Freshman English or little desire to leave a record of his directorship it was, perhaps, because administering the course was not an aspect of his work which stood out from the others or one with which he identified strongly. By his own accounting, Murray estimates that he allocated about 1½ hours per week to the Freshman English Committee and about five hours to his duties as director. These allocations can be contrasted with the number of hours he spent advising students (five),[51] serving on the college Promotion and Tenure Committee (six), teaching (thirty-one), and engaging in professional & scholarly activity (twenty-two). These numbers suggest that service obligations *other than* running the college writing program could take up nearly as much of Murray's time as administering Freshman English.[52] In sum, then, and given his frankly astounding level of ser-

---

50   Of course, it is likely that Murray was required to write reports on Freshman English each year, but if he did these are not in his archive. Again, a curious omission.

51   While this number may seem excessive, Murray notes in numerous of his annual reviews the amount of time he spent advising both undergraduate and graduate students, many of whom were not, technically, his advisees. His student evaluations confirm that Murray was incredibly generous in this capacity, guiding students on questions about career paths, helping to set up and coordinate internships, and providing references for employers.

52   Notably, Murray continued to serve as the de facto administrator of English 501 while he directed Freshman English. ("Faculty Annual Report, 1973–74").

vice commitments during these years,[53] Murray may have seen his work as Fresh-man English director as just one among many responsibilities and obligations at the college and not a career defining role as many WPAs view their work today.

Documents written by Murray's successor in Freshman English, Thomas Carnicelli, paint a vivid picture of his (Murray's) impact on the program and the degree to which his work in English 501 anticipated a revised curriculum for English 401. In a short piece penned for the UNH Parents Association around 1976, Carnicelli identifies "the heart" of Freshman English as "the individual conference between student and teacher." "In a conference," he explains, "the student and the teacher sit down together and discuss the student's paper in detail. We find this a much better way of responding to student papers than the old method of writing copious, often unreadable comments in red ink." Acknowledging the unorthodox nature of this approach, Carnicelli explains that the conference method had proven "highly effective" and was one of the elements of Freshman English that students commented upon most favorably in course evaluations ("Freshman English at UNH").

Another "special feature" of Freshman English at UNH circa the mid to late 1970s that can be traced to Murray was the course's emphasis on revision or what Murray often called, in his early days, "rewriting." As Carnicelli explains, Fresh-man English's "emphasis on revision as an essential part of the writing process" is a hallmark of the UNH approach. Students, he writes, "come to us expecting to write a new paper every week and to have every paper graded. We see no educational value in doing things that way." Instead, he explains, Freshman English instructors envision students' weekly papers as "drafts, not finished products." If a draft shows potential, the instructor will help the student pursue it further. If not, the student will be free to move on to something else. "Professional writers revise the same piece time and time again," Carnicelli points out, "but student writers are rarely given the same opportunity." In Freshman English, he continues, they will be given the chance to write and revise "without the constant pressure of grades," which will be assigned at the end of term, another Murray innovation ("Freshman English at UNH").

Finally, near the end of his letter, Carnicelli addresses the elephant in the room in the teaching of Freshman English: grammar instruction. Here he largely

---

53   Here's a full accounting of Murray's committee assignments from his 1971–1972 annual review (the first year he served as Freshman English director): The Graduate Council, Promotion and Tenure Committee (College of Liberal Arts), Student-Designed Major Committee (chair), Athletic Council, Advisor to *The New Hampshire* student newspaper (therefore de facto member of the university Board of Governors), Graduate Committee (English Department), Freshman English Committee (chair), Personnel Committee (English Department), Committee for the EPDA Junior College Program. "I was disastrously over-committed," Murray notes, of his commitments that year, "although I rejected many [additional] assignments."

reiterates Murray's approach, as articulated in numerous of his early publications. "Many people," he acknowledges, "feel that 401 should place heavy emphasis on the study of grammar." While good grammar is important, he concedes, "first things should be taken care of first. Before a student can even begin to write a decent paper, he or she must find a subject, something to say." Once this is accomplished instructor and student can work together to address additional higher-level concerns such as clarifying one's audience and purpose, developing an organizational structure, constructing an appropriate tone, etc. "Only late in the process of revision," Carnicelli explains, "do we focus our attention on grammar, [at which point] we often find the grammar problems have disappeared" ("Freshman English at UNH").

In Carnicelli's parent letter, but also in his Freshman English guidelines and other administrative documents, we find clear indications of his predecessor's influence. But it's not just Carnicelli. As we saw in the epigraph above from then-Freshman English director Gary Lindberg, over a decade after Murray had moved on from running Freshman English it was still possible to trace the program's vision to him. "If there is a philosophical core to the Freshman English program at UNH," Lindberg writes in the opening lines of his Freshman English manual circa 1985, "it is that we treat our students as writers and our staff as teachers. There is no subject matter the students are being led through, no 'knowledge' they must absorb. Instead, we want them to experience what writing is all about" (Teaching Freshman English).

A trove of Freshman English syllabi from 1987, the year Murray retired from the university, confirms Lindberg's assertions. Virtually every one of the twenty-five syllabi I examined from that fall term requires students to purchase one of Murray's two textbooks. Every syllabus describes the requisite five pages per week of new or revised writing. Every syllabus articulates the weekly conference requirement. And every syllabus describes important pedagogical aspects of the class that can frequently be traced back to Murray's vision. One syllabus describes a central purpose of the course as "to introduce you to the idea of writing as a means of discovering and ordering ideas and information." Another touches on the importance of revision, defining the concept as "a complicated and involved process which alters and (hopefully) improves the structure, thoughts, organization, language, etc. of a piece of writing." A third highlights an aspect of Freshman English that was consistent across all sections at this time: student choice in defining a topic. "A writer's first task," explains the author of this syllabus, "is to find something to write about, and choosing a topic will generally be up to you."

Murray's colleague and friend at UNH, Andrew Merton, who directed Freshman English in the early 1990s, perhaps best articulates how the "philosophical core," as Lindberg put it, stayed true to Murray's intentions, even in the years after his (i.e., Murray's) retirement from the university: "We set out to teach our students to become authorities, to engage their readers, and to revise," Merton writes in a 1992 pamphlet directed to the entire UNH community ("Freshman English"). "To do this, we must get our students to think of themselves, not as students, but as writers." As Merton's words suggest, twenty years after Murray directed Freshman English at UNH his successors were still defining the basic work of the course largely on his terms.

CONCLUSION

Murray wrapped up his work as Freshman English director in the spring of 1974, having served in the post for just three years (he did not teach the course during his tenure as director and only taught it once more before his retirement). During the 1974–75 academic year Murray served as Faculty Chairperson of the entire university. The following year, in the fall of 1975, he became English Department chairman, a post he held for two and a half years, just shy of one term, stepping down prematurely for reasons I'll go into in the next chapter. His years as chair were important and surprisingly productive given the time and energy his administrative commitments undoubtedly required. In his 1975–76 annual review, written in the spring following his first year as department chairman, of his "Professional and Scholarly Activities" Murray writes:

> The University of Buffalo invited twelve "authorities" in the English-speaking world to investigate areas in the writing process and point out the direction research should take in the years ahead. Half-a-dozen of us at a time spent a week-end at Buffalo giving our paper and responding to other papers. This was an exciting and stimulating time for me, and the paper I gave, "Internal Revision: A Process of Discovery," has been well received and has led to further invitations. It will be a chapter in a book to be published by the National Council of Teachers of English.
>
> The paper led to an invitation to participate in a seminar at Rutgers University, and the paper given there, "Teach the Motivating Force of Revision," is scheduled to be a chapter in another book.
>
> The Buffalo paper led Dr. Richard Lloyd Jones of the University of Iowa to ask me to participate in a seminar on theoretical problems in rhetoric at the Conference on College

Composition and Communication in Philadelphia. The paper I gave there, "Reading for Surprise," further develops some of the ideas proposed at Buffalo, and is being prepared for publication.

I was also invited to give a major paper and to participate in a seminar at the Secondary School English Conference of the National Council of Teachers of English in Boston. These papers allowed me to develop my ideas further on the process of internal revision and the implications for teaching.

Ten years earlier, untenured, untested, and still new to academe, Murray had reported to department chairman Jack Richardson on his initial efforts to persuade local high school teachers to reconsider their approach to composition pedagogy (Memo to Jack Richardson). Now, in 1976, he narrated the trajectory of his scholarship—the invitations to share papers, the research seminars with authorities in the field, the pending publications—like an academic rock star. "Although I have planned a role within the group of academics who are investigating the writing process during the last ten years," Murray writes, "I received more professional recognition of that role this year than I have in the past." "My most satisfying work," he continues, "has been in my continuing exploration of the writing process and how to teach it" ("Faculty Annual Report, 1975–76").

With his NESDEC collaborations in the rear-view mirror, his term as Freshman English director over, and his stint as English Department chairman concluded, Murray could have moved on from reform work in the late 1970s and returned to his finally fulfill his creative writing ambitions. Instead, he entered a new period of professional growth and development as a teacher and scholar of composition as the writing process movement gained steam all around him, including at UNH, and as a growing community of writing researchers, with their social science-based investigations into "process," caught up to him.[54]

As we will see in the next chapter, in the late 1970s and throughout the 1980s, with the help of numerous others, Murray doubled-down on his efforts to reform composition pedagogy, in large part due to the emergence of this new "group of academics" who had joined him in investigating the writing process. He greedily immersed himself in the new writing research and worked to find ways to contribute to it in his own unique way. At home, at UNH, he helped

---

54   My phrasing here is intentional and reflects Murray's own sense of how things unfolded. Writing about the second edition of *A Writer Teaches Writing* in the Preface of the revised second edition, Murray writes "I had extended my investigations into how published writers created their drafts and how that information could be shared with students. In addition, I had been joined by many other teacher-researchers who were exploring the same territory and instructing each other" (xi–xii).

launch initiatives that transformed UNH from a *writer's* university and a writing *teacher's* university into a writing *researcher's* university. Having defined himself as an outsider within English, where discussions of pedagogy were not to be entertained, Murray was an immediate insider within the gathering writing process movement, finding, in a new generation of writing researchers, a community of like-minded writer/teacher/scholars with whom to investigate writing, its learning and its teaching.

CHAPTER 4.

JOINING THE WRITING RESEARCH CONVERSATION, 1977–1987

> Until the 1960s the teaching of composition was traditionally performed by the literature faculty, but then composition began to become a discipline of its own, with its own research, scholarship, professional associations and publications, its own professional heritage and teaching methods. The University of New Hampshire was a leader in this new discipline and pioneered the process approach to the study of composition.
>
> – Donald Murray, English 501 Report

> My own revelations, perhaps better called confessions, are merely the speculations of one writer, and they should be suspect. They are not conventional research findings . . . I am not a researcher. I am a writer and a writing teacher. I realize better than my critics how eccentric this may be, but I hope it can be a starting place for more authoritative research.
>
> – Donald Murray, "Reading While Writing"

If central developments impacting Donald Murray's work during the first half of his second career were his collaborations with NESDEC and his work reforming the teaching of writing at UNH (and beyond), a critical context of his work during the second half of his second career occurred with the rise of the writing process movement, nationally, and, locally, at UNH. As numerous disciplinary historians have shown, the 1970s, what Henze et al. dub "that formative decade in the development of composition studies" (4), was a critical period of growth in and expansion of the modern field. Daly Goggin describes the 1970s (and 1980s) as a time when teachers and scholars of writing began to shift their attention away from "practical and pedagogical issues in writing instruction (i.e., the 'what I did' and 'how we do it here' projects)" and towards empirical and theoretical efforts to try to understand "discursive practices and learning processes more broadly conceived" (79). Such a "search for explanations," as Berlin has called it, would require new mechanisms for studying writing and writers. Accordingly, in the 1970s and 1980s new journals were created, new conferences held, new doctoral programs established, and new professional organizations born. Daly Goggin captures a sense of the significance and magnitude of these changes in her assertion that composition and rhetoric became during these years a *wissenschaft*, i.e., "an endeavor for creating knowledge" (103).

In this chapter, I explore Donald Murray's work at UNH and his changing role in composition during its early *wissenschaft* period, from the mid 1970s to the mid to late 1980s (Murray retired from UNH in 1987). During these years, as composition and rhetoric evolved, Murray did too. His primary questions, however, remained largely the same: What happens when writers write? And how can we draw on this knowledge to inform writing's teaching? Anyone offering new answers to these old questions had Murray's ear, including and especially his colleagues at UNH, which became, from the mid 1970s on, a nationally recognized site of innovation in composition research. By 1987, a robust community of writers, teachers, and scholars had grown up around Murray at UNH. While he would always maintain that Carroll Towle was the originator of UNH's writing tradition, for most who came to the university and, more broadly, to the field from the 1970s on, it was Murray, but also, as we will see, his friend and colleague Donald Graves, who were responsible for UNH's modern writing tradition. Murray and Graves, the "Dons" as they were called, were at the center of all that was writing at UNH from the mid 1970s through the early 1990s (Graves retired in 1992).[55]

In this chapter, I begin by exploring the Dons' work together and the process by which they put UNH on the map as a center of research and scholarship in composition and literacy. I then move on to examine Murray's late-career efforts to adapt and contribute to the emergent conversation in composition and rhetoric about writing and its teaching as the field (and he) evolved in the direction of *wissenschaft*.

"THE TIME IS NOW"

While UNH had long been an institution with a special devotion to writers and the teaching of writing, largely of the "creative" sort, it wasn't until 1973, when Donald Graves arrived as a faculty member in the Education Department, that the university became, in the area of writing, a knowledge-*creating* institution in

---

55   Born just six years apart (Murray first) in towns located less than an hour from one another in southeastern Massachusetts, The Dons were both poor students who struggled in school and were, as a result, skeptical of education, traditionally conceived. Both came to the professoriate late, Murray, as we have seen, after a first career in journalism, Graves following careers as a schoolteacher and administrator and as an educational minister. The nature of their work together was such that by 1984, when Murray set about writing a second edition of *A Writer Teaches Writing,* he added an additional dedicatory note to Graves, thanking him for the opportunity "to learn to write and teach" together. A decade later, Graves returned the favor, dedicating his book *A Fresh Look at Writing* to Murray, whom he called "a writer's writer."

the traditional sense of the term. As we see in the second epigraph above, Murray understood that his own work represented only "the speculations of one writer." Graves, however, was a researcher first and a writer second—a researcher of children's literacy, to be exact, whose 1973 dissertation on the composing processes of seven-year-olds won NCTE's Promising Researcher award. Ten years later his field-changing book *Writing: Teachers and Children at Work* won NCTE's David H. Russell Award. Graves was nothing short of a superstar in the field of children's literacy and his presence at UNH was both affirming and sustaining for Murray, who found in him a colleague with the knowledge and skill to carry out the kinds of research of which he was incapable, but had long argued was needed in the field. Graves' arrival in Durham was among the most significant events in Murray's professional life and among the most important moments in the process by which UNH became an institution devoted not just to the teaching of writing but to its study, as well.

Murray and Graves' collaborations began around 1975 when Murray invited Graves to travel with him to participate in the seminars at Buffalo and Rutgers mentioned in the last chapter. Graves returned the favor by enlisting Murray in an early research project with teachers in Peterborough, New Hampshire. A key event that shaped the trajectory of their work together, however, occurred in early 1976, when they appeared on a local radio station to address the controversy brewing nationally and in New Hampshire over *Newsweek's* cover story, "Why Johnny Can't Write." The phone lines were so busy with New Hampshire callers wanting to discuss the nation's "literacy crisis" that the original half-hour show was extended an additional thirty minutes and then, when the hour was up and the phones were still ringing, concluded with a promise that the Dons would return another day to continue the conversation (Center for the Study).

It would be hard to overstate the significance of "Why Johnny Can't Write," in New Hampshire and beyond, to discussions of literacy education and research in the 1970s (see Varnum for a detailed discussion of the article and the crisis it manufactured).[56] The article instigated a climate of animosity in America where teachers and schools were blamed for students' supposed illiteracy and yet it also created an opportunity for teachers, scholars, and other stakeholders to press for change in literacy education and to professionalize in response to a shared threat (i.e., conservative pedagogical retrenchment). According to Henze et al., in the wake of "Why Johnny Can't Write" teachers and scholars of writing worked to increase attention to "remediation, process, and individualized

---

56   As Maureen Daly Goggin points out, a full two decades after "Why Johnny Can't Write" was published it was still being anthologized and new books were still appearing invoking the crisis it created (107).

curricula" (24). Perhaps most famous of those to catch the spirit of this moment was Mina Shaughnessy, who delivered her "Diving In" speech at the December 1975 meeting of the MLA, just weeks after "Why Johnny Can't Write" was published (Maimon in Henze et al. 56). Walker Gibson, too, found, in the "public brouhaha about literacy" "Why Johnny Can't Write" manufactured a kairotic moment for literacy reformers and urged teachers and scholars to seize the opportunity "to do something useful, to make the teaching of writing, both in school and in college, a respected activity" (Gibson, qtd. in Henze et al. 72).

At UNH Murray and Graves heeded Gibson's advice. In early March 1976, just weeks after their radio appearance, Graves penned a memo to his department chair and to Murray, in his capacity as English Department chairman, to make the case for the creation of a new center on campus for the study and promotion of writing, its study, and its teaching. "Over the last six months," Graves writes, "unusual focus has been placed on the writing habits of Americans in school settings." To date, however, media coverage has been "highly negative" and centered on "entirely the wrong issues." Specifically, too much attention has focused on what Graves calls "the accidents of discourse" while "the processes used to create effective writing" have been "left in the dust." Having identified the problem, Graves proposes a local solution: since UNH possesses "unusual resources in both the English and Education departments" they should collaborate to create a center for the "better understanding and application of good writing." "There is a readiness to deal with this in public education," Graves writes. "The time is now" (Proposed Writing Process Center).

That spring The Center for the Study of the Writing Process, later known, simply, as The Writing Process Lab, was established as a joint venture between English and Education. With Murray tied down by his responsibilities as English Department chairman and Graves the rising star in literacy research, it was he (Graves) who served as the center's first director. According to early correspondence the Lab would serve as a place for faculty to come together to discuss "the writing process and writing research." Further, it would disseminate findings of university researchers to the wider state and national community and provide resources to teachers and school districts on writing and writing pedagogy. "Members of the laboratory travel throughout the United States and abroad sharing research data through speeches, workshops, and publications," an early history of the Lab explains, describing work that was carried out largely by Graves, whose reach in evangelizing trumped even Murray's, carrying him to Canada, England, Australia, and New Zealand (Graves "A Short Review"). By the mid to late 1970s, then, spurred on by the *Newsweek*-fueled literacy-crisis, *both* Dons were on the road, preaching the gospel of process to congregants in the U.S. and abroad.

"A CONTRIBUTION TO THE DEVELOPMENT OF A PERSON"

While Murray played a largely behind-the-scenes role in the birth of the Writing Process Lab his contributions were still significant as he supported Graves in his efforts to get the center off the ground and offered critical input and advice along the way to its founding. And Murray was, once the lab was established, an eager participant and active member. Critically, Murray was also involved in early efforts to secure funding for the lab, which commenced around late 1976/early 1977 when he and Graves met with representatives from the Ford Foundation to discuss grant opportunities. These efforts yielded fruit in 1977 when Ford awarded Graves a grant to investigate what he called "the imbalance between sending [i.e., writing] and receiving [i.e., reading]" in literacy research and teaching (5). A year or so later Graves published the results of his investigations in *Balance the Basics: Let Them Write*, written as a direct response to *Newsweek's* "Why Johnny Can't Write" (Murray served as a paid consultant on the project). More than a little Murray can be found in this report and so I'd like to linger on it for just a moment to give a sense of Murray's influence on Graves, but also because Graves' work in researching and writing the report was a critical early development in the process by which UNH expanded its existent writing tradition into the area of research.

In *Balance the Basics,* Graves takes an entirely different tack in discussing the literacy challenges facing the nation from that taken by the authors of "Why Johnny Can't Write." "People want to write," he announces in the very first sentence of the report. "The desire to express is relentless" and yet "most of us are writing less and less" (4). Why? "People do not see themselves as writers," Graves argues, believing that "they have nothing to say that is of value or interest to others." This, he argues, is because in school students are taught that writing is largely "a form of etiquette" in which one's primary job is to "arrange words on paper to avoid error" (4). For Graves, then, the concern facing the nation was less a generation of so-called "semiliterates," as the authors of "Why Johnny Can't Write" argued, than it was an educational system which failed to tap into students' intrinsic desire to express and communicate. If, for the authors of "Why Johnny Can't Write," the literacy crisis was about the "accidents of discourse" found in the writing of too many of the nation's high school graduates, the problem for Graves in *Balance the Basics* was the schools that stifle the creation of literate and engaged citizens. "People want others to know what they hold to be truthful," Graves writes in *Balance the Basics.* "They need to detach themselves from experience and examine it by writing. They need to share what they have discovered through writing. They need the sense of authority that goes with authorship." Schools, Graves argues, with their outdated curricula and ineffectual teaching methods, rob students of the possibility of authorship and the sense of empowerment that follows. "Writing," he asserts, in a sentence that nods to Murray and captures the ethos of the larger movement in which they both were key participants, "is important not as etiquette, not even as a tool, but as a contribution to the development of a person, no matter what that person's background and talents" (6).

Beyond speaking back to traditionalist arguments about literacy development advanced in "Why Johnny Can't Write," Graves also argues in *Balance the Basics* for a new approach to composition pedagogy, what he calls the "process-conference" approach, which, he asserts, will empower students to achieve authorship and its benefits while simultaneously bringing balance to literacy curricula. "The main task of the teacher," Graves writes, "is to help students know what they know" (22). One accomplishes this, he explains, by initiating brief but frequent conferences with students *during* the writing process, rather than by "assigning topics in advance of writing" and making corrections "after the work is finished" (19). The emphasis in this approach is on helping students "discover what [they] know" and then guiding them through multiple drafts which help to "amplify and clarify" a topic. In the end, Graves explains, the overarching purpose of a conference-process approach to composition pedagogy is to help the student develop "the sense of knowing and authority" that is "valuable to any learner" (22).

Published in 1978, five years into his tenure at UNH, *Balance the Basics* played a significant role in the process by which Graves' gained stature in the writing process movement and contributed to UNH's growing reputation as a key site in writing research. And as we have already seen, there is a good deal of Murray in the report. Murray can be found in the claim that children will write easily and copiously if freed from the constraining apparatus of traditionalist literacy instruction. He can be heard in the argument that teachers who don't write will not teach writing well. His presence can be felt in Graves' analysis of the problems of teacher-education programs (i.e., they privilege instruction in teaching reading over teaching writing). And he can be detected in Graves' characterization of the current state-of-affairs as regards writing pedagogy (i.e., "teaching etiquette"). Finally, Murray is there in Graves' over-arching articulation of the purpose for teaching writing in the first place, i.e., personal empowerment and the development of authority. In sum, in *Balance the Basics* we find numerous echoes, and in some cases direct restatements, of arguments Murray had, by 1978, been making for well over a decade.[57] For his part, Murray seems not to have minded or have

---

57 Murray played an essential behind-the-scenes role in the report's writing, as this brief anecdote illustrates: In the early stages of drafting *Balance the Basics*, Graves experienced intense writer's block. Murray gave him a cardboard box that was taped shut, but with a slit cut into the top. Graves was to deposit his writing in the box at the end of each day and deliver it to Murray

been troubled by Graves' borrowing or by the fact that his name appears nowhere in the report (a curious omission). "In all my investigations into the writing process," Murray writes in his 1975–76 faculty annual report, "Dr. Graves has been a stimulating colleague. He has taught me a very great deal. . . . His work and mine has become closely intertwined [sic], and his status on this campus has been extremely important to my work" ("Faculty Annual Report, 1975–76").

GROWTH OF *WISSENSCHAFT* AT UNH

In *Balance the Basics*, as we have seen, Graves makes the case for reform in the teaching of composition and greater parity between funding for reading and writing research. He was immediately effective in the latter as he was awarded, later that year of 1978, a $240,000 National Institute of Education (NIE) grant (nearly $1 million in today's dollars) to conduct a three-year study on children's writing that became the basis for his book *Writing: Teachers and Children at Work*.[58] Based on comments Graves makes in his final report to the NIE, Murray appears to have played some role in this project but was not a primary participant in carrying out the research or a significant partner in writing the book (Graves, "A Case Study" 3–4). While Murray and Graves collaborated on numerous ventures during their years of work together, they maintained, except for a single co-authored article,[59] largely separate research and writing agendas. At the local level, however, they worked closely to expand UNH's writing profile in the direction of *wissenschaft*.

Beyond the creation of the Writing Process Lab, an early development in this regard came in the spring of 1982 when Graves' education department put forward a proposal for the creation of a doctoral program in reading and writing instruction, a combined effort of education, English, and psychology. In making the case for the program, the proposal's authors point to the fact that UNH was now "recognized as one of the major centers for the study of writing in the United States and Canada." To substantiate this claim they point to numerous sources of evidence, including inquiries UNH received from prospective students wishing to study with Murray and Graves; letters from colleagues

so he could read it that night and give feedback for the next day's work. This approach worked and soon Graves was relieved of his writer's block, having found a way to write himself out of the "dissertationese" he had been producing prior to getting Murray's help. (Newkirk, "Why Donald Graves Matters" 4).

58   Graves' career is easily deserving of its own book-length investigation, but none has been forthcoming. Thomas Newkirk and Penny Kittle have published an excellent edited collection of his work, however, *Children Want to Write: Donald Graves and the Revolution in Children's Writing*.

59   See "Revision: In the Writer's Workshop and In the Classroom."

around the country and the world expressing interest in coming to UNH to spend summers and sabbaticals; calls and notes from alumni in and around New England wishing to pursue advanced graduate study at the university; and informational inquiries from the numerous K–12 teachers around New England who had come to expect "both research data and the continuing opportunity for involvement" in literacy research from UNH. In highlighting these requests, the proposal's authors clarify UNH's growing reputation among writing and literacy scholars at this time (Proposal for a Doctor of Philosophy in Education).

And yet, the rise of research in writing did not lead to the decline in teaching of writing at the university. In fact, the opposite happened. Research and teaching, theory and practice, went hand-in-hand as writing faculty doubled-down on efforts to extend and expand the university's commitment to teacher education and outreach. Perhaps most visible in this regard was a 1980 grant Thomas Newkirk secured from the National Endowment for the Humanities (NEH) to launch the New Hampshire Writing Program (NHWP), a summer institute for K–12 teachers held at UNH for the first time in the summer of 1981 (and still in existence today).[60] The grant, funded to the tune of $150,000 (or roughly half a million dollars in today's dollars), was an immediate success, attracting the interest of almost two hundred applicants in its first year (for just sixty spots). Building on and extending Murray's earlier approach to professional development, the NHWP focused on making writers of teachers and drawing classroom pedagogies from informed writerly practice, becoming, in the process, a central means by which the university continued to engage with classroom teachers and, now, attracted potential doctoral candidates.

Another means by which UNH expanded its *wissenschaft* mission during these years was the establishment of a second doctoral program, this one in the English Department, in composition. The doctoral program in reading and writing instruction in the Education Department began to accept its first students in 1984;[61] five years earlier, however, Murray, Graves, Newkirk, and others

---

60   Newkirk, the first compositionist to be hired at UNH, joined the English Department in 1977.

61   UNH Education School graduate students had begun to produce theses and dissertations prior to the establishment of the program in reading and writing Instruction. In 1981, for example, Elizabeth Chiseri-Strater defended the first writing-oriented M.A. Thesis, a composing process investigation of the revision strategies of first-year students (in 1988 she defended her dissertation, an ethnographic investigation of the literacy practices of college students). In 1982 and 1983, the first dissertations were defended, one of which was by Linda Rief. By the late 1980s and early 1990s, the number of students defending dissertations had reached its peak. Four were defended per year in 1991, 1992, and 1994, respectively. These were written by now well-known scholars in the fields of composition and English Education, including Bonnie Sunstein, Tom Romano, Danling Fu and Donna Qualley.

in English had begun to discuss the possibility of what they called "pedagogical dissertations" within the department (Memo from Don Murray to Jean Kennard). As early as 1982, advanced graduate students in English at UNH began to take steps towards making composition an area of specialization and by 1984 a new option in writing pedagogy was added to the existing doctoral program.[62] [63] Thus, by the early to mid 1980s, UNH boasted not one but two doctoral programs—one in education, one in English—to train a new generation of composition and literacy researchers and teachers.

A final means by which UNH became, in the words of the authors of the doctoral proposal in reading and writing instruction, "one of the major centers for the study of writing in the United States and Canada," was the creation of a biennial conference, held at UNH each fall, focused on writing research and literacy scholarship. Whereas Murray, Graves, Newkirk, Fisher, and Carnicelli had been holding workshops and professional development seminars on process-oriented approaches to composition pedagogy for years, the first UNH writer's conference, a weekend-long affair held in 1984 and entitled "Relating Reading and Writing in the College Years," aimed at something more. Dedicated to examining "the interactions between the processes of reading and writing" from a variety of perspectives, including "historical, cognitive, biographical, and critical," the conference featured nationally known speakers in composition, including David Bartholomae, Anne Berthoff, and Richard Ohmann, and included sessions in areas such as "Research in Composition," "Theoretical Problems of the Reading/Writing Process," and "Reading and Writing and Other disciplines." The subsequent 1986 conference, "New Directions in Composition Scholarship," continued in this vein, bringing noted compositionists such as Flower, Shirley Brice Heath, and Andrea Lunsford to campus while offering dozens of sessions on a wide-range of scholarly topics including research into writing and literate development across K–college contexts, technical and professional writing, writing across the curriculum, and teacher-education. While composition pedagogy was still an element of these conferences and teachers and instructors from the elementary to the college level did attend, the focus was largely on *wissenschaft*, broadly defined and expansively imagined.

In her lovely remembrance of the period during which the major initiatives described above were developed at UNH, Sunstein recalls "a rich and

---

62   The first composition dissertations were defended in the English Department in 1987. Throughout the 1990s well-known composition scholars such as Sherrie Gradin, Lad Tobin, Bruce Ballenger, Michelle Payne, and Bronwyn Williams successfully defended dissertations in English composition at UNH.

63   The historian Robert Connors joined the UNH English Department in 1983, thus deepening the department's bench in the area of composition and rhetoric.

productive intellectual moment" (121) when writers—of fiction, non-fiction, poetry, journalism, and academic work; teachers—of elementary, secondary, post-secondary, and non-traditional age students; and researchers—of writing, reading, thinking, and learning, came together to create new understandings of literacy and composition. "The Dons are not the whole story in UNH's influence on composition," Sunstein writes, and yet Murray and Graves were either behind or key players in all of the major *wissenschaft* developments at the university during these years. If, in the 1930s, 1940s and 1950s, under the leadership of Dr. Carroll Towle, UNH became a "writer's university," it expanded, during the 1970s, 1980s, and 1990s, under the leadership of the Dons, to become a writing researcher's university, as well.

ADAPTATIONS AND CHANGING ROLES

In early 1978, a semester shy of completing his three-year term as English Department chairman, Murray stepped down from his position.[64] Reflecting on his time as chair he writes,

> In a department as large as ours, as many as 90 persons . . .
> the job of administration is a seven-day-a-week, 12-month-
> a-year operation, during which time the faculty member
> is expected to teach and to publish. I found it a demand-
> ing, debilitating, thankless job. ("Faculty Annual Report,
> 1977–78")

Once free of his chairmanship, Murray cashed in on a delayed sabbatical that spring of 1978, but his time away from campus was still busy as he continued to travel to give lectures and workshops on writing and pedagogy. In March, he gave talks in Connecticut, Massachusetts, and Minneapolis. In April, he was in Cleveland. He was in Berkeley and Burlington in July and Virginia and Connecticut again in August. As to writing and research, Murray worked on his long-unfinished novel, wrote and submitted six new poems for publication, and drafted or revised four articles on writing that spring and summer of 1978, including three of his most significant pieces, "Write Before Writing" (*CCC*, 1978), "Teach the Motivating Force of Revision" (*English Journal,* 1978), and "The Listening Eye: Reflections on the Writing Conference" (*College English,* 1979). It was the time he spent with Graves in the Writing Process Lab, however,

---

64 In a resignation letter to the dean tendered in the spring of 1977 Murray cites "radical changes in governance" as the official reason for his early departure as chair (Letter to Dean Allan Spitz). Elsewhere he cites the "personal abuse" he received from his colleagues as further cause for his decision to step down early ("Faculty Annual Report, 1977–78").

that he seems to have found most valuable. "Since I was released from other responsibilities," he reflects in his sabbatical report, "I was able to pursue areas of academic exploration which became clear because of the intellectual stimulation of many of my colleagues . . . principally from Professor Donald Graves of the Education Department. My travels this year have reinforced my belief that he is doing more than any other single person to explore and understand the writing process" (Sabbatical Report).

When Murray returned to campus in the fall of 1978 he re-engaged with administrative work, assuming the role of chairman of what had now become the English 501 program. "We have 34 sections of the course this year," Murray writes in his yearly review from 1978–79, "30 of them taught by lecturers and teaching assistants" ("Faculty Annual Report, 1978–79"). In addition to serving as English 501 chairperson, Murray's service commitments at UNH continued to expand in these years. In his 1981 review of Murray's performance, his department chair notes that Murray "is presently serving on at least 7 major University and Departmental committees [including] College Promotion and Tenure Committee, the University Master Plan Committee, [and] the President's Committee to review intercollegiate programs" (Annual Evaluation). Murray's travel schedule, too, was considerable during these years, as this sampling of his "endless number of writing workshops," as his chair put it, illustrates:

- August 23: Workshop for administrators of Nashua Public School System, Nashua, NH
- August 24–25: Workshop for writing program in Stamford School System, Stamford, CT
- September 4: Presentation on the writing conference for Freshman English staff, UNH
- September 5: Keynote speech opening day program in the public schools of Townsend, MA
- September 14: Two presentations for undergraduates and graduates at Whittemore School of Business and Economics, UNH
- September 18: Consultant to Ford Foundation study by Cemeral, Inc., St. Louis, MO
- October 4 and 11: Presentations to graduate students in the Institute of Natural and Environmental Resources, UNH
- October 12: Presentation to interns, home economics department, UNH
- October 21: Keynote speaker and workshop director at the South Carolina English Teachers Conference, University of South Carolina, Columbia, SC

- October 30 and November 6: Workshop for language arts teachers, Dover School System, Dover, NH
- November 10–11: Workshop for representatives from 14 colleges in the University of Wisconsin system, Madison, Wisconsin
- November 17: Workshop for Nashua High School English teachers, Nashua, NH
- December 5: Reading, Writer's Series, UNH
- December 7: Panel member, Writing Program Seminar, UNH[65]

In sum, following his brief, unhappy stint as English Department chairman, Murray was not, it seems, prepared to slow down or ease into retirement.[66] Quite the opposite. Amidst his efforts to serve the university; reform the teaching of writing, the field of English and the larger educational system; and help grow the nascent field of composition and rhetoric, a new series of unanticipated opportunities opened up during his post-chair years in what had once been his primary area of interest, journalism.

While Murray had never completely divorced himself from the world of news and newspapers and had taught journalism courses throughout his years at UNH, he found himself back in an actual newsroom for the first time around 1979–80 when he signed on at *The Boston Globe* to serve as a writing coach. This work was, he writes, "of immense professional stimulation" ("Faculty Annual Report, 1979–80"). Beyond satisfaction the work led to a good deal of new consulting gigs in both journalism and journalism education. Of the twenty-five talks or workshops Murray delivered during the 1980–81 academic year thirteen were with groups associated with newspaper work. In October, he traveled to Florida to meet with writers and editors at the St. Regis Paper Company. In December, he was in Connecticut to deliver a talk at the New England Society of Newspaper Editors. In March, he met with writers and editors in Massachusetts and again in Florida. And in late May, he barnstormed Alaska with

---

65   In his 1975–76 Annual Review, in which Murray was asked to estimate the number of hours he spends per week engaged in teaching, research, and service he arrives at the number 74. Having studied his Annual Reviews I am not surprised by this number, but apparently Murray was concerned that his colleagues and superiors might have been, so he included this note as an addendum to his tally: "If I were you I'd be suspicious of the 74 hour week. Don't be. I can document it as an average. I start at seven each week-day, end at 6, spend two hours at least each evening, three at least on Saturday and six at least on Sunday when I'm not traveling—and I do a lot of traveling."

66   In his 1976–77 "Faculty Annual Report," of his never-ending travel schedule Murray writes, "I have been extremely active in working with groups interested in the teaching of writing. . . . I shall continue it because I am evangelical (75%) and because I need to supplement my income (25%), with two and possibly three children in college in the next few years" (Faculty Annual Report, 1976–77).

consulting gigs at the *Ketchikan Daily News, Juneau Empire,* and *Anchorage Daily News.* Murray published his first article about newswriting in 1981 and began drafting what would become his first book about journalism, *Writing for Your Readers,* which he later published in 1983 ("Faculty Annual Report, 1980–81").

In addition to this new work as a journalism coach and consultant, Murray began to write and publish his own news-related pieces again around this time, as well. At first these were just short essays placed in local papers, but in 1983 he published a feature article on wind turbines in *The Boston Globe* that he had researched during a sabbatical spent in Wyoming in 1982. In the years that followed, Murray penned additional features for the *Globe* and then in 1986 was invited to write and publish a regular column, "Over 60" (later, "Then and Now"). Ostensibly about the aging process, "Over 60" ranged over all matter of senior citizen terrain—from visits with grandchildren to memories of early life to the challenges of caring for an ailing partner.[67] At first Murray published the column only monthly, but once freed of the university and its obligations in 1987 he accelerated the pace of his work, publishing weekly until his death in late 2006.

During the years that Murray re-engaged and expanded his professional profile in journalism his commitments to composition and pedagogy continued apace. In 1984, he published his first college textbook, *Write to Learn.* The following year he published a completely revised edition of *A Writer Teaches Writing.* The year following that, 1986, he published a second college textbook, *Read to Write.* In a re-assessment of one of Murray's major articles published during this period,[68] Thomas Newkirk suggests that the years 1978–1988 were an "intellectually productive period" during which Murray made "his most significant contributions to the field of composition" (Newkirk, "Donald Murray and the 'Other Self'" 47).

There at the beginning, when none of the institutional infrastructure for writing research and scholarship existed, Murray found, by the latter years of his career, that he was now surrounded by a growing community of writer/teacher/ scholars interested in pursuing some of the very questions about writing and its teaching that he had been asking since the early sixties. It was a happy development, at least initially. Once a self-proclaimed expert who, in the absence of a body of scholarly knowledge about writing built his authority on the foundation of his experiential knowledge, Murray was inspired, during his final years at UNH, to adapt and evolve as a new generation of writing researchers began to construct a new foundation of scholarly knowledge about composition and its teaching. The expansion of *wissenschaft* in the field during these years forced

---

67   Murray's wife Minnie Mae, about whom he wrote a great deal in his columns, died in 2005 after a protracted battle with Parkinson's disease.

68   i.e., "Teaching the Other Self: The Writer's First Reader."

Murray to rethink his role and identity. In the early 1970s, he had issued his first call for researchers to draw on the methodologies of "the social sciences and the sciences" to "contribute to the study of the writing process" (Murray, "The Interior View" 21). Imagine his surprise, satisfaction, and gratification, in the late 1970s and 1980s, when a proliferation of such research began to appear in the field's literature, pushing Murray into the unfamiliar but perhaps oddly satisfying position of needing to learn from *others* about what happens when writers write. Imagine his astonishment, in 1982, when he became a participant in this new research, himself, teaming up with Carol Berkenkotter to carry out a naturalistic case study of the composing process.[69] In two decades, Murray had gone from a writer *teaching* writing to a writer participating in research *about* writing.

And yet, while Murray was happy to play the "lab rat" to Berkenkotter's "scientist" he was not yet done, in 1982, playing the writer teaching and investigating writing. Far from it. A careful reading of his work during the years Newkirk identifies as having been significant suggests, however, that there was a question weighing on Murray at this time, and that was what role there was for a writer without scholarly credentials to play in a field increasingly comprised of writing researchers. To his credit, and as we will see, Murray discovered several possible answers to this question. He could serve as a participant in writing research, and did, with Berkenkotter and, a few years earlier, with Graves. He could serve as an advocate for various disciplinary causes, including, in one publication, the need for readable research reports ("Write Research to Be Read") and, in another, the need for greater respect within English for writing program administrators and instructors ("The Politics of Respect"). He could serve as a publishing guide and mentor, sharing the secrets to his writerly success with teachers and scholars who wished to increase their scholarly output ("One Writer's Secrets"). He could serve as a commentator and prognosticator, taking stock of key developments in the field and offering predictions about its future ("REFLECTIONS: The Child as Informer" and "Facets: The Most Important Development in the Last Five Years for High School English Teachers of Composition"). He could serve as an academic scout (perhaps his favorite late role), pointing the new generation

---

69   Murray relates the humorous details of his participation in Berkenkotter's study in a note included with their article in his edited collection *Expecting the Unexpected*. After hearing Berkenkotter give a talk at a conference he introduced himself and, with a few others, discussed Berkenkotter's research but also that of Linda Flower, whose controlled laboratory studies of the composing process Murray felt failed to account for social or contextual variables that inevitably impact the writing task. "After I had made my case," Murray recalls, "Carol introduced me to one of the other people in the group, Linda Flower" (254). Accordingly, Berkenkotter "called [Murray's] bluff" and suggested they conduct a research study together in which she would investigate his composing process in a naturalistic setting. "I didn't have a chance," Murray recalls, and with that their collaboration was born.

of writing researchers towards potentially fruitful areas of unexplored territory (instances of Murray playing this role are too numerous to count). And he could serve as a kind of educational "exhibitionist," publicly "undressing" his writerly practices,[70] routines, customs, habits, obsessions, anxieties, passions, and fears to reveal to the teachers who continued to flock to his workshops, seminars, and lectures the process by which he used writing to, in his words, follow language towards meaning.

With changes in Murray's role came changes in his thinking and writing, as well. For all that has been written, pigeon-holing Murray into the narrow straight jacket of expressivism, the fact is, as with most of us, Murray evolved a good deal in his thinking over the course of his long career. In what follows, I examine several of his key works from the years 1978–1988. Specifically, I revisit several of Murray's most frequently cited articles from the period, according to Google scholar.[71] Simultaneously, I highlight the ways in which Murray worked during these years to situate his writing within the new social science paradigm that was becoming prevalent in numerous of the field's major journals and publications. The pieces I discuss below illustrate Murray's efforts to adapt and adjust his thinking and writing so as to continue to contribute to the field's literature during his final years of active involvement in it.

WRITING LIKE A RESEARCHER (1978–1988)

Of the several papers Murray reports delivering at professional gatherings in his 1975–76 faculty annual report, "Internal Revision: A Process of Discovery" nicely exemplifies his late-career efforts to contribute to the growing knowledge base of the emergent field. Collected in Charles Cooper and Lee Odell's NCTE collection *Research on Composing: Points of Departure*, "Internal Revision" stands as Murray's most frequently cited piece from the period 1978–1988. In it he

---

70 My diction here is intentionally provocative and intended to be amusingly allusive. Around the time that Murray began publicly "undressing" himself, Graves was coming to be known as a "professional nudist" for his criticism that English teachers were too comfortable "wandering around [their] rooms, fully clothed" while their students were "exposed" via their writing and then criticized by teachers at the very moment they were most vulnerable. There's nothing more upsetting, Graves writes in one memorable articulation of this line of thought, "than to have someone walking around fully clothed in a nudist camp, and that often is the teacher, saying 'Hmnn, well, that's a funny navel', 'Hmnn, didn't the Lord give you a better body than that one?' I think that's immoral" ("Renters and Owners: Donald Graves on Writing," *The English Magazine*, NIE Report Package 474). Murray would not be accused of immorality. If he spent his first years in the field with his clothes on, *telling* teachers what writers do when they write, he spent his final years in the field undressing himself publicly so as to *show* them.

71 Unsurprisingly, his most frequently cited article, which I will not revisit, is his manifesto "Teach Writing as a Process Not Product."

speculates about ideas that would later become codified as important threshold concepts in composition and rhetoric, training his eye, in particular, on what he calls "rewriting," "one of the writing skills least researched, least examined, least understood" and, therefore, "least taught," despite the fact that most writers accept it "as a condition of their craft" (123).

Written for a scholarly, and not necessarily a teacherly, audience, Murray opens "Internal Revision," as any researcher must, by reporting on the results of his literature review and by defining his key terms, i.e., internal and external revision. "Although I believe external revision has not been explored adequately or imaginatively," he writes, "it has been explored." As such, he will concentrate his efforts on "attempting to describe internal revision, suggesting opportunities for research, and indicating some implications for the teaching of writing" (131). Internal revision, as Murray explains it, differs from external revision in that the latter focuses largely on "editing and proofreading" as the writer prepares to share his/her work with an audience whereas the former entails a process whereby the writer "use[s] language, structure, and information" to find out what he/she has or hopes to say (130). With internal revision, "the audience is one person: the writer" and the purpose is "discovery." The latter part of this is the idea, articulated by Heidi Estrem in the threshold concept "Writing is a Knowledge-Making Activity," that writers "don't simply think first and then write," they "write to think" (19) or, in this case, write and rewrite to think. It's a notion captured, as well, in the threshold concept "Revision is Central to Developing Writing," in which Doug Downs explains that "while writing, writers usually find something to say that they didn't have to say before writing" (66). Much of Murray's work in "Internal Revision" (and before, and beyond) anticipates these two threshold concepts.

Murray's article "Writing as Process: How Writing Finds its Own Meaning" offers a second useful illustration of his efforts to contribute to the project of the new writing researchers during the latter years of his career. The lead essay in NCTE's collection *Eight Approaches to Teaching Composition*,[72] "Writing as Process," which Murray presciently describes in his 1978–79 faculty annual report as "a major piece of work," anticipates yet another of the field's contemporary interests, knowledge transfer ("Faculty Annual Report, 1978–79"). In this piece, Murray's second most-cited article from the era, he is interested in identifying

---

72   In his 1983 review of *Eight Approaches*, James C. Raymond argues that Donovan and McClelland were wise and correct to make Murray's piece the book's lead. Murray is "a superb writer" Raymond writes, and unlike other journalists who move into composition with "disdain for theory and pedagogy," Murray is, he writes, "well-informed, scholarly, and as inventive in theory as he is admirable in performance" (228). So enamored of Murray's contribution to the collection is Raymond that he argues that it "alone would be worth the price of the book" (229).

and articulating a transferable model of the writing process that, as he puts it, can be "adapted by our students to whatever writing tasks face them" (26).[73] Towards these ends he identifies three steps or stages he suggests most writers pass through most of the time when composing: rehearsing (a term he borrows from Graves), drafting, and revising. What's new here, aside from the fact that pre-writing has been replaced with rehearsing, is Murray's recent understanding of the recursive nature of the writing process. When it comes to the steps or stages of composing, he writes, "We are talking about a process of interaction, and not a series of logical steps" (7). Murray points to the work of Perl as having influenced his thinking in this regard. Before Perl, he confesses, he thought that writers move through the three steps in a roughly linear fashion. After Perl he came to understand that there is an "instantaneous moving back and forth" between the steps or stages of composing (10). Minute by minute, Murray writes, echoing Perl, the writer may be "looking back and looking forward" (10).

Having explained this change in his thinking Murray then goes on to build on and extend Perl by examining the four forces that he claims, "interact as the writing works its way towards its own meaning," i.e., writing, reading, collecting, connecting (11). He returns, in the end, however, to the claim he made in the beginning: "There is no clear line [in the writing process] between the stages of rehearsing, drafting, and revising" (17). It's a correction about which, it seems, Murray wanted the record to speak clearly and it's one of at least two important reversals he made during his career (the other being his understanding that the process writers follow during composing is situationally dependent). In the end, while Murray's portable or transferable model of the composing process likely seems antiquated to our contemporary ears, it serves, nonetheless, as an important illustration of one theorist's early attempt to investigate a key contemporary concern of the field.

As I noted earlier, following Murray's death Thomas Newkirk and several others offered critical reconsiderations of several of his key works (see, for example, Qualley; Ballenger). Newkirk focused on "Teaching the Other Self: The Writer's First Reader," published as the lead article in the May 1982 issue of *College Composition and Communication*. This is another late-career piece that nicely illustrates Murray's efforts to reposition himself as a writing researcher in the spirit of Graves, Perl, and others. As Newkirk reminds us, the task Murray gives himself in "Teaching the Other Self," his third most cited article from the period, is to speculate about what he (Newkirk) calls the "dialectic" between the "self" that writes a text and the "other self" that reads and monitors the text as

---

73   As we have seen earlier, this is the riddle that Murray spent most of his career trying to unravel.

it's being written (Newkirk, "Donald Murray and the 'Other Self'" 48). The term monitoring, used repeatedly in "Teaching the Other Self," calls to mind Murray's interest in explicit reflection. In "Teaching the Other Self," he revisits this interest as he works to describe the numerous metacognitive functions "the other self" performs while "the self" composes. These include acting as a "supportive colleague to the writer," playing the role of the "critic," and serving as a project manager to observe, organize, and make sense of the writing process as it unfolds (142). In his articulation of "the other self," Murray anticipates several important contemporary threshold concepts, including and especially Charles Bazerman and Howard Tinberg's "Text is an Object Outside of Oneself That Can Be Improved and Developed." "Becoming aware that the text exists outside the writer's projection and must convey meaning to readers is an important threshold in developing a more professional attitude toward the act of writing and what is produced," Bazerman and Tinberg write (61). It is this, precisely, that Murray wishes to convey to his readers in "Teaching the Other Self," an article that, despite its theoretical focus, also has a good deal to say about pedagogical matters. In helping student writers gain awareness of and cultivate their "other self," Murray asserts, teachers will help them on their journey to develop "more professional" attitudes and dispositions towards writing. Initially, the teacher may have to play the role of the other self because, as Murray warns, students "may not know that the other self exists" (147). Over time, however, and with careful mentoring, students can be made aware of the other self's existence, learn of its value, and experience the gains in writerly productivity that its cultivation can enable.

Beyond Murray's efforts to contribute to the emergent composing process research of the seventies and eighties by theorizing from his own experience and observations, nothing may signal his commitment to and interest in the field's new investigations more than his participation in an actual study of composing process research. Twenty years into his career, Murray's involvement in Carol Berkenkotter's naturalistic research offered him the opportunity to make visible to someone else that which he had been examining himself all those years. The resultant article, "Decisions and Revisions: The Planning Strategies of a Publishing Writer," with an addendum, "Response of a Laboratory Rat—or, Being Protocoled," is Murray's fourth most cited piece according to Google scholar. "In the absence of more proper academic resources," he writes in his addendum, "I have made a career of studying myself while writing." When Berkenkotter asked him to "run in her maze," he reports, he "gulped" but "did not think [he] could refuse" (169).

Berkenkotter's sixty-two-day deep-dive into Murray's writing process contributed to and extended the work of previous writing researchers in at least two important ways.[74] First, it was the first study to investigate a professional writer composing in a naturalistic, as opposed to a laboratory, setting. Second, it was the first study to combine think-aloud protocol analysis with the writer's own testimony or account of composing, thus allowing the participant a voice in the research process, a crucial step forward in the ethics of writing research. The study yielded interesting results but also shed light on what Berkenkotter calls Murray's "distinctive work habits" (159):

> Unlike most writers who hand draft or type, Mr. Murray
> spends much time making copious notes in a daybook, then
> dictates his drafts and partial drafts to his wife, who is an
> accomplished typist and partner in his work. Later, he reads
> aloud and edits the drafts. If he determines that copy-editing
> (i.e., making stylistic changes in the text) is insufficient, he
> returns to the daybook, makes further notes, and prepares for
> the next dictation. (158–59)

Having studied Murray intensively for two months Berkenkotter offers several interesting observations about his methods, the most notable of which, perhaps, is her finding about the role of audience-awareness in Murray's process. *Audience* is not a word Murray used with great frequency in his writing about writing, preferring, instead, the perhaps more journalistic term *reader*. A full consideration of readers and how their needs shape all aspects of the composing process was not typically a primary interest or concern for Murray, though. As we saw in "Internal Revision," Murray frequently conceived of writing as a process whereby the needs of readers enter into the composing process rather late, after the essential details of discovering meaning and purpose are already worked out. For Murray, the exigence for writing almost always originated within the writer and his or her need to communicate, and this makes a kind of sense, especially given Murray's experience as a freelance writer prior to his transition to college teaching. That a writer's meaning and purpose might be shaped, first and foremost, by the needs of his/her audience was not a way of thinking about writing that Murray wrote a great deal about or in which he seemed much interested.

And yet it's this, precisely, that Berkenkotter discovered when she peaked behind the curtain of Murray's composing process: Murray *did*, in fact, think about audience, about his readers, during the writing process, and she goes so

---

74   It's worth pointing out that Murray, himself, conceived of the project as an extension of the work of others, writing, "we have developed a method for studying professional writers under naturalistic conditions, something that has not been done before, and extends the pioneering work done by Flower and Hayes at Carnegie Mellon University" (Faculty Annual Report, 1981–82)

far as to call him out on this point in her article where she asserts that writers do not "only consider their audiences when doing external revision." Rather, as she explains, writers' awareness of audience shapes their writing and revisions to a significant degree in the beginning, middle, and at the end of a writing project. Some of Murray's most significant revisions, in fact, "occurred as he turned his thoughts toward his audience" (166). Humbled but perhaps still in disbelief, Murray speaks to this point in his "Lab Rat" follow up. "I was far more aware of audience than I thought I was during some of the writing," he concedes. "My sense of audience is so strong that I have to suppress my conscious awareness of audience to hear what the text demands" (171). Perhaps. Or perhaps Murray was so aware of audience because in all acts of writing such awareness is essential to discovering the available means of persuasion (and reversing one publicly is always hard).

In his addendum to Berkenkotter's article, Murray makes clear his sense of what he thinks their work together contributes to the field. "What I think we have done, as rat and ratee," he writes, "is to demonstrate that there is a process through which experienced writers can be studied under normal working conditions on typical writing projects. I think my contribution is not to reveal my own writing habits but to show a way that we can study writers who are far better writers than I" (172). There is, of course, a paradox here. Murray's criticism of composing process research published before his and Berkenkotter's study, a criticism that led to his collaboration with Berkenkotter in the first place, was that in placing writers in labs and giving them artificial writing tasks, the authors of these studies failed to account for the social or "naturalistic" contexts that shape composing. As Berkenkotter puts this, echoing Murray, "If we are to understand how writers revise, we must pay close attention to the context in which revision occurs" (156). The irony, of course, is that a writer who would soon be criticized for failing to account for the role of context in composing wanted to make sure that writing researchers would account for the contexts which shape the composing of their research participants.

CONCLUSION

The years 1978–1988 were a period during which Murray made some of his most important and interesting contributions to the growth and development of composition and rhetoric—locally, at UNH, and nationally, on the lecture circuit and in the pages of the field's growing literature. Simultaneously, Murray re-engaged with his roots in newswriting during, discovering yet another new professional role, journalism coach, and a new outlet for his writing (i.e., his *Boston Globe* column). He retired from UNH in 1987, having served on the faculty for 24 years, just shy of a quarter century. His relationship with UNH, however, extended back forty-four years, to the time when he was briefly stationed at the university for basic training ahead of his deployment to Europe during World War II. "The Army delivered me to Durham, by train, in 1943," Murray recalls in his final annual report to the university in the spring of 1987. "I was marched to my dormitory on Main Street. . . . I applied to be admitted to the University if I returned from the war. I felt this was a place where I could write and learn to write." Of his time as a student at UNH in the forties, Murray writes, professor Carroll Towle and other members of the English Department faculty inspired him to "question, doubt, speculate, to learn in response to my own questions." Of his time as faculty member from the sixties through eighties he expected, he explains, that he would be a teacher, but found that he was a student—of his own and his students' learning. "And the university allowed this," he writes, with evident astonishment and satisfaction. In the years ahead, in his retirement, he forecasts, he intends to become a "student emeritus" as he continues to learn his trade (Annual Report for the Academic Year of 1986–87). Murray made good on this promise—writing, speaking, and publishing on writing and its teaching until his passing in late 2006.

Death, it seems, was the only thing that could put an end to his evangelizing.

CONCLUSION.
A REFORMER'S LEGACY

> While all the other pioneers in composition tended to move from the outside in, Murray moved from the inside out.
>
> > – Robert Root, "Donald Murray Remembered"

> I imagined in the sixties that I would lead an army of writers into the academy, that they would take composition research and teaching seriously, and that they would be taken seriously. Together we would begin to understand how effective writing is made, and our new knowledge would change what we teach and how we teach it. . . . It's harder now that there is a body of scholarship, though, a canon guarded by high priests. The profession has no place for writers, and writers have no interest in the discipline that does not seem to relate to them or what they do. Writers are not taken seriously. Writing researchers do not think writers have anything to contribute. . . . I know of virtually no studies going on now on how people write. This is a personal disappointment to me.
>
> > – Donald Murray, "'Mucking about in Language I Save My Soul': An Interview with Donald Murray"

> I think that for me, what was so important was the feeling that we were democratizing writing. So, as opposed to writing being this skill that only a narrow subset of people have, writing is something that everybody has, or can have. I still think that was a great revolution.
>
> > – Thomas Newkirk, "Democratizing Writing: Reflections on The Great Revolution"

This book was born of the fear that Donald Murray's legacy in composition and rhetoric has been written by those who either didn't know him, didn't read him carefully, read him too selectively, or read him largely to advance their own agendas. I'm not the first to want to recover, resuscitate, and reclaim Murray, however. Other UNHers, in particular, have come before me. I stand on the shoulders of folks like Bruce Ballenger, Lad Tobin, Tom Newkirk, Donna Qualley, Bronwyn Williams and many other members of what I have called, elsewhere, my UNH "tribe" (Michaud, *Notes of a Native Son*). Writing in 2008, shortly after Murray's death, Tom Newkirk articulates the anger and frustration many of us have felt at the way Murray was so easily reduced to the *Donald Murray = Expressivist* frame and summarily dismissed. "I am unconvinced that Don's work can be so neatly aligned with a particular ideology," Newkirk writes. "[Murray] appealed to a huge range of writers, of varying political orientations. These writers appropriated from it [sic] what they needed." He continues,

> Now, after twenty years, "expressivism" has been part of the vocabulary of composition studies, a frequently used shorthand that dissolves the complex work of Murray and others into a compact position that in my view was never accurate in the first place. It can lead to intellectual reductiveness, to assertions that there really is this "rhetoric" that to my mind no thinking person would really subscribe to. It marginalizes and diminishes—to the point where I suspect Murray would be totally unknown to emerging professionals if *Cross-Talk* didn't have a four-page essay, written in the early 1970s. My hope is that he might be given a second look, a good rereading. ("Donald Murray and the 'Other Self'" 51)

Here, in addition to pushing back against the *Donald Murray = Expressivist* frame, Newkirk provides the exigence for the project I have pursued in these pages: to recover and reinterpret Murray. I have gone beyond "a good rereading," however, turning to microhistory for my reclamation project. According to Ginzburg, "The specific aim of [microhistorical] research should be . . . The reconstruction of the relationship . . . between individual lives and the contexts in which they unfold" (Ginzburg qtd. in McComiskey 17). In these pages, I've tried to put these elements into conversation, situating the story of Murray's individual life within the contexts—personal, institutional, professional, disciplinary—in which it unfolded. In so-doing, I've asked readers to move beyond the "grand narrative" of *Donald Murray = Expressivist* to a more nuanced understanding of Murray's life, work, and contributions to our field, to conceive of him *not* as synonymous with a single approach to composition pedagogy but, rather, as a complex figure in our field's disciplinary history whose efforts to reform the teaching of writing, the discipline of English, and the larger educational system of which both are a part should be understood and celebrated.

Of course, Murray didn't set out in life to become a reformer. He set out to *write* and he spent a lifetime doing so. Once the opportunity to work for change presented itself to him in the early 1960s, however, he swam with the current, sometimes hesitantly and even, at times, reluctantly, but at a consistent and steady pace for the entirety of the second half of his career, through his retirement, and right up until his death. "Each time I sit down to write I don't know if I can do it," Murray wrote in the final column he published in the *Boston Globe* while still alive. "The flow of writing is always a surprise and a challenge. Click the computer on and I am 17 again, wanting to write and not knowing if I can" ("The Past Present and Future" C3).

Once in the reform current there was so much Murray wanted to change—about writing pedagogy, about English, about schools. It has taken me an entire book to try to articulate both *why* I believe he labored at this work for so long and *how* (and with whom) he went about it. Regarding the former, the *why*, as I have argued Murray's motivations were often personal, an act of "revenge," as he occasionally put it, on the teachers who "inspired [him] to drop out of high school twice before flunking out" (*My Twice-Lived Life* 32). Within the field of English, he conceived of reform, similarly, as a kind of revenge, but against English teachers and professors who enacted a version of the discipline that Murray understood to be not just mistaken in its conceptions about writing and writers but actually damaging to students trying to learn to write. Regarding the latter, the *how*, as we have seen Murray's process of working for pedagogical, educational, and disciplinary reform was anything but systematic. Around 1964, in response to a very local exigence at UNH, he put his head down to try to understand how his own writing process worked and to ask what implications an examination of this process might suggest for those who teach writing. From this effort flowed numerous arguments about writing and its teaching and, as we have seen, countless attempts at operationalizing these arguments in the form of specific reforms, on campus at UNH and beyond. But could Murray have imagined, in the summer of 1963, as he prepared to take a position as a faculty member and journalism instructor at his old alma mater, that five years later he would no longer be writing nonfiction articles for general interest audiences but, instead, writing about writing for school teachers? Could he have imagined, in the fall of 1971, when he assumed the directorship of Freshman English, that five years later he would be sought out by scholars in the emergent field of composition and rhetoric to deliver papers at research seminars? Could he have imagined, in the winter of 1978, when he stepped down as English Department chairman, that five years later (and almost twenty years after he had first begun to examine his own writing practices) a scholar trained in social science research methodologies would come to his house for 62 days to study his writing process and report on her findings in one of the field's major journals? Finally, could he have imagined, in 1986, when his article "One Writer's Secrets" was published as the lead piece in *College Composition and Communication*, that five years later an essay he penned for a special issue of the same journal would be relegated to the "Staffroom Interchanges" section (more on this in a moment)? No, Murray could not have imagined any of these developments before they happened, a fact which he acknowledges himself in a lovely passage from his memoir *My Twice-Lived Life*. Murray recalls the day his eldest daughter, nearing her college graduation, sat him and his wife down to ask how they had planned their lives. "We laughed and said that we had not planned our lives," Murray explains, "it was all an accident" (49). Later in the book he reflects, "In a lifetime I had moved from being one of the dumb kids sitting in the back row, to standing behind the teacher's desk, to teaching teachers. I have, indeed, lived an unexpected life" (14).

MOVING FROM THE INSIDE OUT

One of the most unexpected and unfortunate aspects of Murray's professional life seems to have been, as Robert Root put it in the first epigraph above, his movement in the late 1980s and 1990s from composition's "inside out." Murray spoke the words in the second epigraph, above, during an interview conducted with the journal *Writing on the Edge* (*WOE*) in 1993, five years out from his retirement from UNH. The words *disappointed* and *disappointment* appear frequently in the transcript. During a moment when Murray and the editors are discussing his feelings of alienation from the field he says, "I'm disappointed in what's happened but I'm not the least bit surprised. . . . When you professionalize inquiry, produce and hire professionals, you get professionals. I could not have been hired to replace myself when I retired, I didn't have the education" (13–14). Murray had not retired from composition and rhetoric but had come to feel that he *had been* retired by the field. Still, he was grateful for the changes that had made him obsolete. "I wanted people to do research in the teaching of writing," he explains. "I fought for our becoming a discipline" (14).

What Murray didn't want and what increasingly concerned him in his latter years were what he perceived to be the downsides of the field's evolution, one of which he felt personally and the other of which registered more as a professional concern. As we learned in the last chapter, Murray's "eccentric" speculations on the writing process were, as the eighties approached the nineties, no longer treated with the same level of seriousness as they once were by the field's new gatekeepers. "Scholars put me in a funny pigeon hole where I feel uncomfortable," he explains in his interviewers at *WOE* (13). To illustrate he offers an anecdote about a recent experience he'd had trying to place an article in one of the field's leading journals. Before eventually finding a home for the piece elsewhere, Murray explains, it was turned away from the first journal to which he submitted it for being "too Murrayesque" and rejected by the second, which, he reports, had invited the piece, for being "quaint" (29). "I wish my article was better written," Murray reflects on this incident, "that's normal enough for a writer—but it is not normal to wish his writing was dated, yesterday's news, old-fashioned, perhaps even what an article of mine was called in a recent journal rejection: 'quaint.' It is not. Not yet" ("Author's Postscript" 87).[75]

---

75 As late as 1990, some in the field still found Murray's unique approach to composition scholarship useful. In a review of his edited collection *Expecting the Unexpected*, for example, Susan McLeod writes, "These essays illustrate what is most outstanding about Murray's work:

Beyond his feelings of personal disappointment, the changes in the field which stirred in Murray professional frustration stemmed from his sense that in its arc of disciplinary evolution, composition and rhetoric had shifted its primary research focus away from the kinds of inquiry and investigation into writing that he felt were most needed (i.e., studies of writers writing) and towards something else, what he calls, in one instance, "all the political and social issues that always surround writing" ("Author's Postscript" 88). Ten years on from his stint as a "Lab Rat," Murray reports that he was increasingly unable to find research reports that built on and extended his and Berkenkotter's project in meaningful ways. "I would like to see close, precise examinations of the writing act," he asserts in his interview with *WOE*. "How do people write? How do the best students write? In any class, whether you're teaching in a prison or a remedial class in the inner city or rural schools, there are students in the class who write better than others. Where do they get their ideas? How do they revise? How much do they do in their head and on the paper?" (20). As we see here, Murray's questions in 1993 hadn't changed that much since 1963, and yet the field had changed a great deal. "Does the profession think that those questions have been answered," the editors of *WOE* ask, "Or did it get frustrated with the difficulty of answering them?" Murray's response reveals the depths of his frustrations at this time: "The profession today is not interested in writing. It is interested in grand ideas around writing, in political issues, in ethnographic issues—all valuable—not what happens when one word collides on the page and unexpected meaning is born." Further, he adds, damningly, "I don't think the profession tried to answer the questions enough to get frustrated" (21).

Acting on his disappointment and frustration, Murray never again published in a mainstream journal in the field following the 1991 publication of his essay "All Writing is Autobiography" in *CCC*. In a short retrospective piece he penned in 1993 for the journal *North Carolina English Teacher,* revisiting his 1977 article "Our Students Will Write—If We Let Them," he writes, "The smaller, 'less professional' journals, such as *NCET*, that remain close to the public-school classroom, are the places where the profession is surviving. This is where I believe new research on how writers write and how students learn to write will be published" (88). In the dozen or so years that followed, Murray acted on this assertion, only placing his writing about writing in venues like *NCET* or in edited collections published by friends and colleagues in the greater UNH writing community. If those who wielded influence in composition and rhetoric's halls of power no longer found his evangelizing compelling, Murray would look elsewhere for congregants.

---

he has the ability to engage us personally as he reveals his experiences in war, his pain at his daughter's death, his joy and frustration and vulnerability in writing and in teaching writing. He may not be a researcher, but he is certainly a writer, and a splendid one. Our discipline is richer for the introspective accounts of his work" (418).

THE LABOR OF MINNIE MAE MURRAY

During the editorial review process for this book one reviewer noted, with curiosity, the following line, quoted in the last chapter, from Carol Berkenkotter's research report: "Mr. Murray spends much time making copious notes in a daybook, then dictates his drafts and partial drafts to his wife, who is an accomplished typist and partner in his work" (158). Like my reviewer, I have found much to scratch my head about in this formulation, beginning with the anachronism "an accomplished typist" and ending with the descriptor "partner." During my research, I, too, became curious about Minnie Mae Murray and her role in her husband's work. Was she more *typist* or more *partner*? A belated but much-needed word is in order here, as this book winds down, about the professional aspects of the Murrays relationship.

References and allusions to Minnie Mae can be found throughout Murray's writing and descriptions of her contributions to his work are recounted in numerous of his publications. Murray was, if nothing else, consistent in publicly recognizing, thanking, and praising his wife and in acknowledging her role in his work and success. In many instances in which he mentions Minnie Mae in his earliest UNH communications, it is to bemoan the uncompensated work she does for the university. In a seven-page rant to his department chairman about other matters, Murray pauses to go into some detail describing Minnie Mae's labors on behalf of the department and university:

> Perhaps this is the time to bring up another question. Other faculty members of equivalent rank and energy and activity have secretaries. So do I. Perhaps she should be paid by the university. We have a large, well-equipped office established with private funds. Minnie Mae was an executive secretary who has a high professional price on her head. She spends many hours each day on university business. We have to hire people to do some of her housework for her so she can do this. A good share of what she does is administrative work for the university, another part of what she does is preparation for my courses, and another part, probably, is university sponsored research. . . . We have not worried about this, because her life is integrated with mine, and because we have not separated artificially the work I have done for the university and for myself. (Letter to Jack Richardson).

Murray's claim about Minnie Mae's unpaid contributions to UNH is corroborated in a report on the work of a general education committee on which he served as secretary in the late 1960s, in a passage where the report's authors acknowledge the "Help of a different, but equally important" kind that committee members received, "from [their] families." Here, Minnie Mae, and *only* Minnie Mae, is named: "One wife, Minnie Mae Murray, did double duty by acting as secretary to the committee's secretary. Our excellent minutes were the labor—not always of love—of the Murrays" (Toward Unity Through Diversity).

Minnie Mae's contributions to Murray's work at the university were not confined to his service commitments, however. In an interview Murray gave late in his life, he provides a vivid illustration of the extent of her contributions to his writing and research. "The first draft of *Write to Learn* was written as we drove from New Hampshire to Kentucky to see Minnie Mae's mother," Murray recalls. "Minnie Mae had a typewriter in front of her on a little desk in the van and I dictated all of it" (Boe and Marting 8). Further, as we learned from Berkenkotter, Murray's "distinctive work habits" (159) were both unusual for an academic and highly collaborative.[76] He wrote extensive notes in his journal or "daybook" and then dictated early drafts to Minnie Mae (sometimes, apparently, in the car, on vacations). Once a draft was completed, Murray read it aloud to determine whether it should be copy-edited and published or whether he needed to return to his daybook to consider more substantial revisions.[77] If the latter, there was more work, yet, for Minnie Mae Murray to do.[78]

While Murray never quite goes into detail on the specifics of Minnie Mae's intellectual contributions to his work, it's clear from statements he makes in various places that she was, in the end, more *partner* than *typist*. In a 1964 letter proposing story ideas to his editor at *Reader's Digest* Murray writes, "I think I would be a far more efficient reporter and writer if I were able to move right into the

---

76   Coming to higher education from private industry, as Murray did, it's not entirely surprising that he would have grown accustomed to writing by dictation. Further, throughout his life Murray struggled with spelling and so, in an era before the advent of spell and/or grammar checkers, having Minnie Mae type up his early drafts likely saved time and ensured correctness. For her part, administrative work was nothing new to Minnie Mae as she had served, according to her obituary, as a secretary to the scientific advisor to the Secretary of War during World War II (and, in so doing, had earned the nation's highest security clearance!). ("Minnie Mae")

77   If the document he was writing covered ideas Murray had already rehearsed in speeches, seminars, or workshops, Berkenkotter reports, the writing process went fairly quickly. In just a draft or two Murray had a relatively polished copy. If, however, Murray was breaking new conceptual ground, covering previously unexplored terrain, the process was more laborious and plodding, with multiple iterations of drafting/dictating/typing, reading/rethinking, drafting/dictating/typing, reading/rethinking, and so on.

78   According to Tom Newkirk, once word processors came on the scene in the 1980s, Murray abandoned dictation and took to the keyboard to handle typing his manuscripts himself (Email Correspondence, 12/6/22).

area where I am reporting. I would have my office and my secretary-researcher (my wife) with me." Later in this letter he writes, "My wife is a good reporter, and so am I. As we travel the country we would inevitably come up with story ideas, far more than we could ever utilize." (Letter to James Monahan). Here, Minnie Mae is named as both a *researcher* and a *reporter*, terms that suggest the nature of her partnership with her husband prior to and during the early years of his transition to college teaching. Given Murray's lone-wolf status when he worked as a freelancer, we should perhaps not be surprised at such a partnership and it was likely during those years that, as Murray put it above, Minnie Mae's professional life became "integrated" with his.

On the dedications and acknowledgments pages of Murray's many books we learn about additional roles Minnie Mae played in his work. In *A Writer Teaches Writing*, for example, he acknowledges Minnie Mae's contributions, which, he reports, "go far beyond the chore of typing and re-typing and retyping . . ." (xiv). In the Preface of *Learning by Teaching*, Murray is more expansive on the support Minnie Mae provided him, of the emotional sort:

> Most of all, I appreciate the support of my wife, Minnie Mae,
> to whom all of these pieces have been dictated, not once, but
> many times. She is the one who has seen the despair caused
> by all the false drafts, and if it were not for her support, that's
> all there would be, just early drafts of articles I would some
> day hope to write.

Did Minnie Mae go beyond emotional support to make intellectual contributions to Murray's work? In the dedication for his book *Writing for Your Readers* he deploys a term, *reader*, which suggests she surely did. "For my First Reader, Minnie Mae," he writes. The term appears again years later in Minnie Mae's obituary (which, I speculate, Murray wrote), in a passage in which Minnie Mae is described as "her husband's first reader and first editor." The term *reader*, or, more specifically, *first* reader, suggests that Minnie Mae played an important intellectual role in her husband's work. On the one hand, the term could be interpreted literally, as in, she was the first to read his work because she was typing it. On the other hand, *first* reader suggests a more expansive role, as we designate as *first reader* those individuals whose opinions and judgments we value most. My sense is that Murray intended the latter.

In *Write to Learn*, beyond again dedicating the book to Minnie Mae ("without her there would be no books"), Murray describes his wife as his "closest colleague and strongest supporter" (xiv). It's a long way from *typist* to *colleague*. To be clear, though, it was Berkenkotter who gave us *typist*, and while Murray occasionally used this term himself he also, as we have seen, used numerous other terms to describe

Minnie Mae's contributions to his work: *researcher, reporter, reader, colleague, supporter.*[79] [80] So where does all this leave us on the questions that prompted this brief inquiry into the professional partnership of Don and Minnie Mae Murray?

I think we can say, first, that if we place the Murrays' collaborations within the context of their times they're probably not all that unusual or surprising. Second, we should probably acknowledge and understand Minnie Mae's work for her husband (and the university) as a likely extension of the professional relationship they established prior to the time when Murray transitioned to college teaching. After nine years of working together during Murray's freelance period it must have been fairly easy to continue in this capacity once Murray joined the faculty at UNH (and may even have been necessary, so that Murray could take on the speaking and consulting gigs necessary to earn the additional income the family needed to pay the bills). Third, though, I think that we can acknowledge that when viewed through the lens of our own contemporary moment, the Murrays' work relationship feels problematic. As a twentieth century cisgen white male, Murray worked from a position of considerable privilege . . . and then he also had a wife to support him, providing free labor for numerous years. All of these conclusions feel valid. Most significant, though, is the fact that the Murrays remained married, and happily so, by all accounts, until Minnie Mae's death in 2005. Whatever we might say about it, their professional work arrangement seems to have worked for them.

DEMOCRATIZING WRITING

Donald Murray came to UNH in 1963 with two novels under his belt and a contract for a third in hand. He never published that third novel, but it wasn't

---

79   And to this list one can also add *caterer, hostess,* and *chef,* as the Murrays frequently entertained faculty and students at their home and Minnie Mae, of course, organized and presided over such gatherings. Such was the extent of Minnie Mae's culinary competence, in fact, that she was sometimes named in Murray's teaching evaluations (asked to comment on the aspects of the course that were the most successful, one student points to "Minnie Mae's cooking").

80   Towards the end of her life, Minnie Mae played a final, significant role in her husband's work: *muse.* While Murray set out in his *Boston Globe* column, initially, to document his own aging process his reporting took a more focused turn in the 1990s when Minnie Mae was diagnosed with Parkinson's disease. At this time Murray became her full-time caregiver and his writing increasingly charted the challenges of caring for a partner with a debilitating and life-altering condition. As such, especially during the early years of her illness, Minnie Mae became something of a minor celebrity among Murray's *Boston Globe* readers. "When her husband gave readings," Minnie Mae's obituary notes, "the audiences were most interested in seeing Minnie Mae." True or not, it's clear that throughout his career Minnie Mae played an essential role in Murray's accomplishments and success.

for lack of trying. Five or so years into his time at the university, as he drafted and field-tested *A Writer Teaches Writing*, Murray was still at work on the third novel, for which, he reports, he still had a contract ("Faculty Annual Report, 1967–68"). A few years later, in 1970, as the list of his publications and speaking engagements in the area of writing and pedagogy grew, Murray provides the following update in his annual report on the novel-in-progress: "developed conceptually, but not close to publication. Hope for completion in 1971." While this hope did not come to fruition, as we learn from Murray's 1973–74 annual report, the novel at least now had a name, *The Ghosting of Manton Blake*, and while it is listed third in order of significance under his Professional and Scholarly Activities, it is, Murray explains in the report, his "principal writing project at the moment." The following year, however, we learn that the novel was still unfinished. The update: "Since the last report I have written approximately 80,000 words on a draft of a novel. This draft has been reconsidered and largely abandoned, but it is an essential part of the novel in progress, which I have reconsidered and reorganized."

Perhaps unsurprisingly, progress on the third novel slowed during the years Murray served as department chairman. Further, it was at this time that he drifted further away from more mainstream forms of writing, gaining greater attention among composition researchers as he experimented with more social scientific modes of composing. In a 1977 sabbatical request, however, Murray indicates that if granted leave he hopes to devote much of his time and energy to completing the novel "for which I have a contract and which I have delayed by serving as chairperson." And then, happily, in a report for the year 1977–78, Murray indicates that he now has "a firm outline for the entire work" and "should be able to fill in that outline during this academic year." The following year, for the first time, the novel, now entitled *Ghosting*, is listed as "Completed" in Murray's Annual Report.

Completed, but apparently not publishable, for *Ghosting* receives no mention again in Murray's Annual Reports until 1983. "4th and final draft to be delivered Spring 1983," he writes, but elsewhere in his report he indicates that he's now at work on another project, called *My Military History of the Twentieth Century*. In the years that followed, Murray appears to have ghosted *Ghosting* because the book does not appear again in his reports, replaced, now, by frequent references to *My Military History*, for which, he explains in 1988, he has both a contract and five completed chapters. Among his goals for 1990, he writes, is to finish *My Military History* (Annual Report of Don Murray for 1988). And yet, even though there is ample evidence in his archive that Murray continued to labor on "the novel" from 1990 until his death in 2006, he never finished it or, if he did, never published it.

It was very *un*Murrayesque for Murray not to finish something he had started, especially if it was in the realm of writing. "I [first] came to the University as an out-of-state student because of the artistic climate created by Carroll [Towle]," Murray explained in a profile published in the UNH student newspaper in 1964. "I came back to enjoy the same climate" ("I Have to Write" 10). While the climate was not, ultimately, hospitable for Murray to write and publish fiction it did prove amenable for other kinds of creative writing, mainly poetry. Beginning around 1970 or so, Murray began (or resumed) writing poems and was soon placing them in both mainstream publications like *The New York Times* and literary journals like *The Southern Poetry Review*. "I have completed 23 poems this year, which are being submitted for publication," he writes in the spring of 1975 ("Faculty Annual Report, 1974–75"). Virtually every year thereafter similar such announcements followed. "Twenty-eight poems completed, ready to be sent out at year end," he writes in 1988. The writing (and publishing) of poems, it seems, was more conducive to Murray's frantic, even manic, pace once he began to work towards disciplinary and educational reform.

Why did Murray continue to labor at fiction and poetry long after his bread and butter had become writing about writing? One possible answer is that throughout his life Murray never confined himself to just one type of writing. He got his start penning simple news stories, advanced to editorial writing, and it was for this that he won the Pulitzer Prize. In the fifties and early sixties, he made a living writing features for general interest magazines and then, of course, in the late sixties and early seventies he transitioned into a kind of hybrid academic/essayistic genre of writing that earned him tenure and promotion and a name for himself in the emergent field of composition and rhetoric. In the seventies and eighties, Murray labored to try to find ways to continue to contribute his ideas to the evolving field, often in the form of a kind of quasi-social scientific genre of writing, but he also wrote the occasional newspaper piece and briefly returned to long-form journalism before signing on to become a columnist at *The Boston Globe* (he wrote textbooks, as well, during this period). For the final twenty or so years of his life Murray frequently wrote autobiography, publishing two memoirs and countless columns about his major themes: family and childhood, school and war, parenting and aging. In sum, one answer to the question of why Murray kept writing "creatively" is that there was never really a time in his life when Murray produced just one kind of writing. He always wore many writerly hats and thought of all writing as creative.

A second possible answer to the question is more personal, though. Throughout his life but especially during his formative years, Murray dreamed of becoming a capital "W" Writer and it was this, specifically, as we have seen, that he had initially set out to accomplish when he signed on to teach at UNH. We should not be surprised, then, that Murray continued to pursue this goal during his years on the faculty, even as more immediate academic projects drew him further and further from it. We should also not be surprised to find that Murray sometimes struggled to come to terms with the trade-offs he was making as he pursued these unanticipated writerly projects. "My credentials are certainly not academic, and neither are my ambitions," he wrote to a friend circa 1970, seven years into his new life as a college professor. "I still want to be a writer-writer, not a writer-about-writing" (Letter to Mr. Walter Holden). The following year, in a brief personal reflection on his career, Murray opens with the following: "In my mind I am a writer and a teacher of writing—in that order" (Professional Reflection). Finally, in a lengthy, meandering letter written around this same time to his friend and sponsor at NESDEC Dick Goodman, Murray acknowledges his feelings most directly: "Probably I should confess something that is hard to understand. I can not accept the writing I do about writing—the books, articles, and programs—as writing. I should, but I can not" (Letter to Richard Goodman).

In his late-life book *Crafting a Life in Essay, Story, Poem*, Murray blames his English professors for instilling in him an outlook that assigns greater prestige to so-called "creative" forms of writing. "When I was in college, my professors preached an aesthetic pyramid of literature: poetry at the peak, fiction and drama below, nonfiction at the bottom," he writes. Sadly he "bought it," he admits (55). He learned to value certain genres more than others. And yet there were likely other factors at work, as well, in Murray's allegiance to "an aesthetic pyramid of literature." Murray came of age during a period of great American literary accomplishment. Fitzgerald. Hemingway. Faulkner. Steinbeck. All men, like Murray. All white, like Murray. Some even served in wars or as journalists, as Murray had. It would have been difficult for an aspiring young writer of Murray's generation *not* to get caught up in the mythology of these men, these Great American Writers. It's likely, then, that Murray's inability to give up on creative forms of writing, to give up on the "novel," was not just about what his professors had taught him. Prior to coming to college Murray had already cultivated a writerly persona that was not easily surrendered and this, too, is likely part of the reason why he kept at his novel (and his poems) well past the point at which he had become known, principally, as a writer teaching writing. One does not give up on a long-held and deeply internalized identity just because one changes jobs. Writing novels and poems was identify-fulfillment for Murray, the dream of Writerly fame an unattainable goal whose sole purpose became its pursuit.

As the scales of Murray's life unexpectedly rebalanced in the sixties and seventies, he had pursued a new writerly goal—democratizing writing, as Thomas Newkirk has put it. Making writers out of ordinary folks, and not just a Writer out of himself. In *A Writer Teaches Writing*, Murray writes,

> The writer may be a novelist, a salesman, a lawyer, a historian, a member of the League of Women Voters, an engineer, a journalist, a general, a philosopher, a politician, an advertising copywriter, a union official, a businessman, a scientist. Those categories simply identify the material he has to communicate, they do not indicate whether he is a writer or not. The man who creates an effective memo is as much a writer as the man who produces an effective sonnet. (1)

The notion that "the man who creates an effective memo" is "as much a writer" as "the man who produces an effective sonnet" can be seen as a kind of democratic counterargument or response to what Murray felt were elitist mythologies about writing and writers that had long been perpetuated by non-writers, and especially English teachers and professors, including at UNH. Murray addresses this issue head on in the first edition of *A Writer Teaches Writing* where he writes, "I endeavor to show the students as I write with them that writing is not magic, but work." He continues: "The writer does not put on a velvet smoking jacket, pick up a quill pen and let God direct his hand across the page" (21). Elsewhere, he aims his arguments more directly at those whom he believes peddle the fiction that writers are a special class of people and writing a special kind of skill. "When we teach writing we do our students a disservice if we allow them to think that writing is a mystery. Writing is not a magic possessed only by the high priests of the English Department" (*Instructor's Manual . . . Write to Learn* 23). Regular people, Murray argued, striking a dagger into the dark heart of the rhetoric of liberal culture, could become writers, and he offered his own life as evidence for this claim. To my way of thinking there is no more important contribution that Donald Murray made to our field than this—his tireless effort to deputize all of us, including and especially our students, *as* writers.

To be sure, and as we have seen in these pages, Murray gave us many useful things: maps of the composing process; a vision of writing as a problem-solving activity; an understanding of writing development as a process of lifelong learning; advocacy for the importance of explicit reflection in the teaching of writing; an inductive, listening-based, response-oriented approach to composition pedagogy; arguments for the legitimacy of composition within English; an appreciation for the importance of productive failure in learning to write; and a vision of teaching and learning grounded in joy, pleasure, discovery, curiosity, and surprise. It was Murray's willingness to line up his considerable ethos as a Pulitzer Prize winner behind the notion that writing could be learned and practiced by anyone willing to try, however, that is, I believe, his most enduring legacy.

The irony, of course, is that the enormous amount of time Murray spent trying to democratize writing, to show us not just that the identity of writer was *possible* but that it was *desirable* and even *attainable,* was time he didn't spend becoming the Writer of his dreams. In trying to make writers of us all, Murray largely forfeited his own Writerly ambitions. Or, perhaps he didn't. Perhaps he eventually came to believe the truth of his own words: a man who creates an effective memo . . . or a revolutionary academic article, successful workshop presentation, groundbreaking textbook, innovative curriculum series, or helpful instructor's manual *is* as much a Writer as the man who produces an effective sonnet.

One can hope so.

WORKS CITED

Adler-Kassner, Linda, and Elizabeth Wardle, editors. *Naming What We Know: Threshold Concepts of Writing Studies*. Utah State UP, 2015.

Adler-Kassner, Linda, and Elizabeth Wardle. "Metaconcept: Writing is an Activity and a Subject of Study." *Naming What We Know: Threshold Concepts of Writing Studies,* edited by Linda Adler-Kassner and Elizabeth Wardle, Utah State UP, 2015, pp. 15–16.

Almutared, Abdullah Mohamed Zareb. "English Writing Strategies in Al-Diya Secondary School: A Case Study of Third Secondary Class." *The Arab Journal of Educational and Psychological Sciences*, vol. 2, no. 3, 2018, pp. 319–27.

Al Sabiri, Almakki Rumadhan, and Sibel Ersel Kaymakamoğlu. "A Study on the Views of English Literature Teachers about How to Teach English Literature: Libyan Higher Education Context." *Folklor/Edebiyat*, vol. 25, no. 97, 2019, pp. 391–406.

Anderson, Carl. "Individualize Writing Instruction by Conferring with Your Student Writers." NESA Fall Training Institute, 8–9 Nov. 2019, Riffa Views International School, Riffa, Bahrain. https://www.nesacenter.org/uploaded/conferences/FTI /2019/Handouts/CarlAnderson_Conferring_NESA_2019.pdf.

"Annual Evaluation: Donald Murray, Full Professor." May 1981. *Donald Murray Collection.* The Milne Special Collections and Archives, University of New Hampshire, Durham.

Babcock, Donald. *The History of the University of New Hampshire, 1866–1941.* The Record Press, 1941.

Ballenger, Bruce. "Reconsiderations: Donald Murray and the Pedagogy of Surprise." *College English*, vol. 70, no. 3, 2008, pp. 296–303.

Berkenkotter, Carol. "Review." *Rhetoric Review*, vol. 4, no. 1, 1985, pp. 111–15.

Berkenkotter, Carol, and Donald M. Murray. "Decisions and Revisions: The Planning Strategies of a Publishing Writer, and Response of a Laboratory Rat: Or, Being Protocoled." *College Composition and Communication*, vol. 34, no. 2, 1983, pp. 156–72.

Berlin, James. "Contemporary Composition: The Major Pedagogical Theories." *College English*, vol. 44, no. 8, 1982, pp. 765–77.

———. "Rhetoric and Ideology in the Writing Class." *College English*, vol. 50, no. 5, 1988, pp. 477–94.

———. Rhetoric and Reality: Writing Instruction in American Colleges, 1900–1985. Southern Illinois UP, 1987.

Bingham, Sylvester H. "Letter to Dean Edward Y. Blewett." 11 June 1958. *Freshman English Files, 1955–1968.* The Milne Special Collections and Archives, University of New Hampshire, Durham.

Bird, Jennifer Lynne. *Narratives of Patient Care: Using Narrative Writing to Enhance Healing.* IGI Global, 2020.

Bird, Jennifer Lynne, and Eric T. Wanner. *Narratives of Anxiety: Using Narrative Writing to Enhance Healing.* IGI Global, 2020.

Bishop, Wendy. "Places to Stand: The Reflective Writer-Teacher-Writer in Composition." *College Composition and Communication*, vol. 51, no. 1, 1999, pp. 9–31.

Boe, John. "From the Editor: Donald Murray Speaks!" *Writing on the Edge*, vol. 17, no. 2, 2007, pp. 3–9.

Boe, John, and Janet Marting. "An Interview with Donald Murray: 'Lose Yourself.'" *Writing on the Edge*, vol. 14, no. 1, 2003, pp. 7–17.

Bridwell-Bowles, Lillian. "Designing Research on Computer-assisted Writing." *Computers and Composition*, vol. 7, no. 1, 1989, pp. 81–94.

Brodkey, Linda. "Writing on the Bias." *College English*, vol. 56, no. 4, 1994, pp. 527–47.

Bulletin of the University of New Hampshire Catalog Issue for 1925–1926. University of New Hampshire, 1925.

Bulletin of the University of New Hampshire Catalog Issue for 1928–1929. University of New Hampshire, 1928.

Bulletin of the University of New Hampshire Catalog Issue for 1935–1936. University of New Hampshire, 1935.

Bulletin of the University of New Hampshire Catalog Issue for 1942–1943. University of New Hampshire, 1942.

Bulletin of the University of New Hampshire Catalog Issue for 1945–1946. University of New Hampshire, 1945.

Bulletin of the University of New Hampshire Catalog Issue for 1964–1965. University of New Hampshire, 1964.

Bulletin of the University of New Hampshire Catalog Issue for 1966–1967. University of New Hampshire, 1967.

Bulletin of the University of New Hampshire Catalog Issue for 1967–1968. University of New Hampshire, 1967.

Bulletin of the University of New Hampshire Catalog Issue for 1968–1969. University of New Hampshire, 1967.

Bulletin of the University of New Hampshire Catalog Issue for 1969–1970. University of New Hampshire, 1964.

Carillo, Ellen C. "The Evolving Relationship Between Composition and Cognitive Studies: Gaining Some Historical Perspective on our Contemporary Moment." *Contemporary Perspectives on Cognition and Writing*, edited by Patricia Portanova et al., The WAC Clearinghouse/UP of Colorado, 2017, pp. 39–55. https://doi.org/10.37514/PER-B.2017.0032.2.02.

Carnicelli, Thomas. "Freshman English at UNH." *Parenthesis, the Newsletter of the UNH Parents' Association*, vol. 1, no. 2, 1976.

Center for the Study of the Writing Process. *Donald Murray Collection*. The Milne Special Collections and Archives, University of New Hampshire, Durham.

Clifford, John. "Review." *College Composition and Communication*, vol. 39, no. 1, 1988, pp. 99–101.

Combs, Shane D. "Queering Time and Space: Donald Murray as Introvert Whisperer." *Composition Forum*, vol. 37, 2017, https://compositionforum.com/issue/37/queering.php.

Connolly, Paul, and Teresa Vilardi, editors. *New Methods in College Writing Programs: Theories in Practice*. Modern Language Association, 1986.

Connors, Robert J. *Composition-Rhetoric: Backgrounds, Theory, and Pedagogy.* University of Pittsburgh P, 1997.

———. "Dreams and Play: Historical Method and Methodology." *Method and Methodology in Composition Research,* edited by Gesa Kirsch and Patricia A. Sullivan, Southern Illinois UP, 1992, pp. 15–36.

Cook, Gillian E., and Sandra Stotsky. "Review." *College Composition and Communication,* vol. 37, no. 4, 1986, pp. 490–93.

Coomber, Matthew. "A Comparison of Self-Directed Revision Strategies in EFL Writing." *The Asian EFL Journal,* vol. 23, no. 4.1, 2019, pp. 76–105.

Crowley, Sharon. *Composition in the University: Historical and Polemical Essays.* University of Pittsburgh P, 1998.

Daniels, Sharie, and Pamela Beck. "Perceptions of Teacher-Writers: Initial Influences to Write." *Northwest Journal of Teacher Education,* vol. 14, no. 2, 2019, pp. 1–24.

Downs, Doug. "Revision is Central to Developing Writing." *Naming What We Know: Threshold Concepts of Writing Studies,* edited by Linda Adler-Kassner and Elizabeth Wardle, Utah State UP, 2015, pp. 66–67.

Downs, Doug, and Elizabeth Wardle, editors. *Writing About Writing,* 1st edition. Bedford/St. Martin's, 2010.

Dryer, Dylan B., et al. "Writing Is (Also Always) a Cognitive Activity" *Naming What We Know: Threshold Concepts of Writing Studies,* edited by Linda Adler-Kassner and Elizabeth Wardle, Utah State UP, 2015, pp. 71–82.

Dumbrell, Laurel. "Donald Graves: The Professional Nudist." *Education News,* vol. 17, no. 8, 1981, pp. 469–72.

ÉBida, Rosa Dos Santos. *Quality In Brazilian Political Journalism: Coverage of The Process of Impeachment by Dilma Rousseff.* 2019. University of Brasília Faculty of Communication Graduate Program, Ph.D. dissertation.

Estrem, Heidi. "Writing is a Knowledge-Making Activity." *Naming What We Know: Threshold Concepts of Writing Studies,* edited by Linda Adler-Kassner and Elizabeth Wardle, Utah State UP, 2015, pp. 19–20.

Faigley, Lester. "Competing Theories of Process: A Critique and a Proposal." *College English,* vol. 48, no. 6, 1986, pp. 527–42.

Fisher, Lester, and Donald M. Murray. "Perhaps the Professor Should Cut Class." *College English,* vol. 35, no. 2, 1973, pp. 169–73.

Fulkerson, Richard. "Composition Theory in the Eighties: Axiological Consensus and Paradigmatic Diversity." *College Composition and Communication,* vol. 41, no. 4, 1990, pp. 409–29.

———. "Four Philosophies of Composition." *College Composition and Communication,* vol. 30, no. 4, 1979, pp. 343–48.

Gaillet, Lynée Lewis. "Archival Survival: Navigating Historical Research." *Working in the Archives: Practical Research Methods for Rhetoric and Composition,* edited by Alexis E. Ramsey et al., Southern Illinois UP, 2010, pp. 28–39.

Gephardt, Richard. "These Essays on Writing Dispel Myths, Provide Useful Insights." *The Phi Delta Kappan,* vol. 65, no. 6, 1984, pp. 432–33.

Geckle, George L. "The Dual Master's Degree." *ADE Bulletin,* no. 62, 1979, pp. 42–45.

Gilyard, Keith. *Voices of the Self: A Study of Language Competence.* Wayne State UP, 1991.

Gogan, Brian. "Going Public with Ken Macrorie." *Microhistories of Composition*, edited by Bruce McComiskey, Utah State UP, 2016, pp. 256–83.

Goggin, Maureen Daly. *Authoring a Discipline: Scholarly Journals and the Post-World War II Emergence of Rhetoric and Composition.* Erlbaum, 2000.

Gold, David. "Remapping Revisionist Historiography." *College Composition and Communication*, vol. 64, no. 1, 2012, pp. 15–34.

———. *Rhetoric at the Margins: Revising the History of Writing Instruction in American Colleges, 1873–1947.* Southern Illinois UP, 2008.

Goldblatt, Eli. "Don't Call It Expressivism: Legacies of a 'Tacit Tradition.'" *College Composition and Communication*, vol. 68, no. 3, 2017, pp. 438–65.

Goodman, Richard H., and Donald M. Murray. "Project Write: A Proposal to Use the Professional Writer to Improve the Teaching of High School Composition." 3 Aug. 1966. *Donald Murray Collection.* The Milne Special Collections and Archives, University of New Hampshire, Durham.

Gradin, Sherrie L. *Romancing Rhetorics: Social Expressivist Perspectives on the Teaching of Writing.* Boynton/Cook Heinemann, 1995.

Graham, Marlo Anne. *Writing Pedagogy in the Early Years: A Study of Teacher Beliefs, Classroom Practices and Influences.* 2019. Australian Catholic University, Ph.D. dissertation. ACU Research Bank, https://acuresearchbank.acu.edu.au/item/8v72z /writing-pedagogy-in-the-early-years-a-study-of-teacher-beliefs-classroom-practices -and-influences.

Graves, Donald. *Balance the Basics: Let Them Write.* The Ford Foundation, 1978.

———. *A Case Study Observing the Development of Primary Children's Composing, Spelling, and Motor Behaviors During the Writing Process.* Project No. 8-34/9-0963. United States Department of Education, National Institutes of Education, 1981.

———. *A Fresh Look at Writing.* Heinemann, 1994.

———. "In Memoriam: Donald Murray 1993–2006." *Language Arts*, vol. 84, no. 6, 2007, pp. 562–63.

———. "Proposed Writing Process Center." 9 Mar. 1976. *Donald Murray Collection.* The Milne Special Collections and Archives, University of New Hampshire, Durham.

———. "Renters and Owners: Donald Graves on Writing." *The English Magazine*, vol. 8, 1981, pp. 4–7.

———. "A Short Review of the Writing Process Laboratory." 2 Jul. 1985. *Donald Murray Collection.* The Milne Special Collections and Archives, University of New Hampshire, Durham.

Graves, Donald H., and Donald M. Murray. "Revision: In the Writer's Workshop and in the Classroom." *The Journal of Education*, vol. 162, no. 2, 1980, pp. 38–56.

Harrington, David V. "Teaching Students the Art of Discovery." *College Composition and Communication*, vol. 19, no. 1, 1968, pp. 7–14.

Henze, Brent, et al., editors. *1977: A Cultural Moment in Composition.* Parlor Press, 2007.

Herrick, James A. *The History and Theory of Rhetoric: An Introduction*, 6th Edition. Routledge, 2017.

"I Have to Write: A Visit with Don Murray." *The Alumnus*, 1964, pp. 10–11.

Imelda, I., et al. "Process Writing Approach Combined with Video-Based Mobile Learning: EFL Students' Perceptions." iNELTAL Conference Proceedings. The International English Language Teachers and Lecturers Conference, 4–5 Nov. 2019, Universitas Negeri, Padang, Indonesia.

Iowa Writing Project. "Writers Teaching, Teachers Writing: Fall Conference." 13–14 October 1985, University of Northern Iowa, Cedar Falls.

James, Marion. *The University of New Hampshire, 1955–2002: The Rise of Research*. The University of New Hampshire, 2010.

Kerbs, Macie. *The Language and Practice of Writing Teachers: Exploring Teacher Professional Learning*. 2019. Texas Woman's University, Ph.D. dissertation.

Kirsch, Gesa E., and Liz Rohan. *Beyond the Archives: Research as a Lived Process*. Southern Illinois UP, 2008.

Kitzhaber, Albert. *Themes, Theories and Therapy: The Teaching of Writing in College*. McGraw Hill, 1963.

Lakoff, George. *Don't Think of an Elephant!: Know Your Values and Frame the Debate—The Essential Guide for Progressives*. Chelsea Green Publishing Company, 2004.

Larson, Richard. "Editor's Note." *College Composition and Communication*, vol. 37 no. 2, 1986, pp. 145.

Lerner, Neal. "Remembering Roger Garrison: Composition Studies and the Star-Making Machine." *Microhistories of Composition*, edited by Bruce McComiskey, Utah State UP, 2016, pp. 217–36.

Lindberg, Gary. *Teaching English at the University of New Hampshire*. Undated manuscript.

———. "University of New Hampshire Freshman Composition Program." *New Methods in College Writing Programs: Theories in Practice*, edited by Paul H. Connolly and Teresa Vilardi, Modern Language Association of America, 1986, pp. 130–134.

"Literary Contests Nearing Deadlines." *The New Hampshire*, 28 Mar. 1941, no. 4.

Lynn, Steven. "Reading the Writing Process: Toward a Theory of Current Pedagogies." *College English*, vol. 49, no. 8, 1987, pp. 902–10.

Lu, Min-Zhan. "From Silence to Words: Writing as Struggle." *College English*, vol. 49, no. 4, 1987, pp. 437–48.

Maimon, Elaine. "The Birth of WAC." *1977: A Cultural Moment in Composition*, edited by Henze, et al., Parlor Press, 2007, pp. 56–57.

Masters, Thomas M. *Practicing Writing: The Postwar Discourse of Freshman English*. University of Pittsburgh P, 2004.

Mayes, Patricia. "Teacher Authority and the Collaborative Construction of Agency in Second Language Writing Instruction." *Theorizing and Analyzing Language Teacher Agency*, edited by Hayriye Kayi-Aydar, et al., Channel View Publications, 2019, pp. 180–98.

McComiskey, Bruce, editor. *Microhistories of Composition*. Utah State UP, 2016.

———. "Introduction." McComiskey, pp. 3–38.

McLeod, Susan. "Review." *Journal of Advanced Composition*, vol. 10, no. 2, 1990, pp. 417–18.

———. *Writing Program Administration*. Parlor Press/The WAC Clearinghouse, 2007.

Media Education Foundation. "Peter Elbow on Writing: A Conversation With America's Top Writing Teacher." https://www.mediaed.org/transcripts/Peter-Elbow-On -Writing-Transcript.pdf. 1995.

Merton, Andrew. "Freshman English: How it Works (And Why, Sometimes, It Appears Not to)." Undated.

Michaud, Michael. "Composing a Career, from Expressivism to Essayism: A Conversation with Bruce Ballenger." *Composition Forum*, vol 41, Spring 2019, http://comp ositionforum.com/issue/41/bruce-ballenger-interview.php.

———. "Democratizing Writing: Reflections on the Great Revolution, A Conversation with Thomas Newkirk." *Composition Forum*, vol. 32, Fall 2015, https://compo sitionforum.com/issue/32/thomas-newkirk-interview.php.

———. "Notes of a Native Son." *Intermezzo*, 2017, https://intermezzo.enculturation .net/04-michaud.htm.

———. "On The Creative-Nonfiction of Composition and Rhetoric: An Interview with Lad Tobin." *Composition Forum*, vol. 43, Spring 2020, https://composition forum.com/issue/43/lad-tobin-interview.php.

———. "Victims, Rebels, and Outsiders: Reconceiving Donald Murray." *Writing on the Edge*, vol. 25, no. 2, 2015, pp. 51–68.

———. "What We Talk About When We Talk About Donald Murray: Revisiting A Writer Teaches Writing at 50." *Composition Forum*, vol. 40, Fall 2018, http://com positionforum.com/issue/40/murray-retrospective.php.

Michaud, Michael, and Doug Downs. "No, Really: Teach Writing as a Process not Product." *Composition Forum*, vol. 50, Fall 2022, https://compositionforum.com /issue/50/teach-writing-as-process.php.

"Minnie Mae Emmerich Murray Obituary." Legacy.com, https://www.legacy.com /obituaries/name/minnie-murray-obituary?pid=3151490.

Moran, Charles. "How the Writing Process Came to UMass/Amherst: Roger Garrison, Donald Murray, and Institutional Change." *Taking Stock: The Writing Process Movement in the '90s*, edited by Lad Tobin and Thomas Newkirk, Boynton/Cook, 1994, pp. 133–52.

Mueller, Derek. "Grasping Rhetoric and Composition by its Long Tail: What Graphs Can Tell Us About the Field's Changing Shape." *College Composition and Communication*, vol. 64, no. 1, 2012, pp. 195–223.

Murray, Donald. "All Writing Is Autobiography." *College Composition and Communication*, vol. 42, no. 1, 1991, pp. 66–74.

———. "Annual Report for the Academic Year of 1986–87." Undated. *Donald Murray Collection*. The Milne Special Collections and Archives, University of New Hampshire, Durham.

———. "Annual Report of Don Murray for 1988." Undated. *Donald Murray Collection*. The Milne Special Collections and Archives, University of New Hampshire, Durham.

———. "Author's Postscript." *North Carolina English Teacher*, vol. 50, no. 3, 1993, pp. 87–88.

———. "City Boy Finds Woods, World of Book." *Manchester Union Leader*, 25 June 1976, p. A31.

———. *The Craft of Revision*, 5th ed. Wadsworth/Cengage Learning, 2013.

———. *Crafting a Life in Essay, Story, Poem*. Heinemann, 1996.

———. "Dear John Letter." 30 Mar. 1971. *Donald Murray Collection*. The Milne Special Collections and Archives, University of New Hampshire, Durham.

———. "Dominant Impression." *Exercise Exchange*, vol. 17, no. 1, 1972, pp. 3–5.

———. "Donald Murray Revised Chronology." Undated. *Donald Murray Collection*. The Milne Special Collections and Archives, University of New Hampshire, Durham.

———. "English 501 – Expository Writing." 19 Feb. 1971. *Donald Murray Collection*. The Milne Special Collections and Archives, University of New Hampshire, Durham.

———. *Expecting the Unexpected: Teaching Myself—and Others—To Read and Write*. Heinemann, 1989.

———. "The Explorers of Inner Space." *English Journal,* vol. 58, no. 6, 1969, pp. 908–11.

———. "Facets: The Most Important Development in the Last Five Years for High School Teachers of Composition." *The English Journal*, vol. 73 no. 5, 1984, pp. 20–23.

———. "Faculty Annual Report, 1967–68." Undated. *Donald Murray Collection*. The Milne Special Collections and Archives, University of New Hampshire, Durham.

———. "Faculty Annual Report, 1970–71." 23 Sept. 1971. *Donald Murray Collection*. The Milne Special Collections and Archives, University of New Hampshire, Durham.

———. "Faculty Annual Report, 1971–72." 23 May 1972. *Donald Murray Collection*. The Milne Special Collections and Archives, University of New Hampshire, Durham.

———. "Faculty Annual Report, 1972–73." 18 May 1973. *Donald Murray Collection*. The Milne Special Collections and Archives, University of New Hampshire, Durham.

———. "Faculty Annual Report, 1973–74." 21 Mar. 1974. *Donald Murray Collection*. The Milne Special Collections and Archives, University of New Hampshire, Durham.

———. "Faculty Annual Report, 1974–75." 5 May 1975. *Donald Murray Collection*. The Milne Special Collections and Archives, University of New Hampshire, Durham.

———. "Faculty Annual Report, 1975–76." 20 Apr. 1976. *Donald Murray Collection*. The Milne Special Collections and Archives, University of New Hampshire, Durham.

———. "Faculty Annual Report, 1976–77." 14 Apr. 1977. *Donald Murray Collection*. The Milne Special Collections and Archives, University of New Hampshire, Durham.

———. "Faculty Annual Report, 1977–78." 22 Apr. 1978. *Donald Murray Collection*. The Milne Special Collections and Archives, University of New Hampshire, Durham.

———. "Faculty Annual Report, 1978–79." 7 May 1979. *Donald Murray Collection*. The Milne Special Collections and Archives, University of New Hampshire, Durham.

———. "Faculty Annual Report, 1979–80." 4 Apr. 1980. *Donald Murray Collection*. The Milne Special Collections and Archives, University of New Hampshire, Durham.

———. "Faculty Annual Report, 1980–81." 22 Mar. 1981. *Donald Murray Collection*. The Milne Special Collections and Archives, University of New Hampshire, Durham.

———. "Faculty Annual Report, 1981–82." 25 Feb. 1982. *Donald Murray Collection*. The Milne Special Collections and Archives, University of New Hampshire, Durham.

———. "Faculty Annual Report, 1982–83." 1 Mar. 1983. *Donald Murray Collection*. The Milne Special Collections and Archives, University of New Hampshire, Durham.

———. "Faculty Annual Report, 1985–86." Undated. *Donald Murray Collection*. The Milne Special Collections and Archives, University of New Hampshire, Durham.

———. "The Feel of Writing—and Teaching Writing." *Reinventing the Rhetorical Tradition*, edited by Aviva Freedman and Ian Pringle. L & S Books, for the Canadian Council of Teachers of English, 1980, pp. 67–74.

———. "Finding Pleasure in the Challenge of a Blank Sheet." *The Boston Globe*, 26 Dec. 2006, p. D3.

———. "Finding Your Own Voice: Teaching Composition in an Age of Dissent." *College Composition and Communication*, vol. 20, no. 2, 1969, pp. 118–23.

———. "Freshman English Planning Committee Memo." 15 Feb. 1966. *Donald Murray Collection*. The Milne Special Collections and Archives, University of New Hampshire, Durham.

———. "Getting Under the Lightning." *Writers on Writing*, edited by Tom Waldrep, Random House, 1985, pp. 215–24.

———. "Guidelines for English 501, Expository Writing." 14 Mar. 1966. *Donald Murray Collection*. The Milne Special Collections and Archives, University of New Hampshire, Durham.

———. "To Heck with Nostalgia." *New Hampshire Alumnus*. Autumn 1987, pp. 8–10.

———. *Instructor's Manual to Accompany Write to Learn*, 6th edition. Harcourt Brace College Publishers, 1998.

———. "Internal Revision: A Process of Discovery." *Research on Composing: Points of Departure*, edited by Charles R. Cooper and Lee Odell, National Council of Teachers of English, 1978, pp. 85–104.

———. "The Interior View: One Writer's Philosophy of Composition." *College Composition and Communication*, vol. 21, no. 1, 1970, pp. 21–26.

———. "Knowing Not Knowing." *Taking Stock: The Writing Process Movement in the '90s*, edited by Lad Tobin and Thomas Newkirk, Boynton/Cook, 1994, pp. 57–65.

———. "A Landscape of Words." *UNH Magazine*, Fall 2000.

———. "Letter to Dean Allan Spitz." 16 May 1977. *Donald Murray Collection*. The Milne Special Collections and Archives, University of New Hampshire, Durham.

———. "Letter to Dr. David W. Ellis." 9 Oct. 1972. *Donald Murray Collection*. The Milne Special Collections and Archives, University of New Hampshire, Durham.

———. "Letter to Dr. Richard Goodman." 31 Jan. 1970. *Donald Murray Collection*. The Milne Special Collections and Archives, University of New Hampshire, Durham.

———. "Letter to Jack Richardson." 18 Apr. 1968. *Donald Murray Collection*. The Milne Special Collections and Archives, University of New Hampshire, Durham.

———. "Letter to Mr. James Monahan." 7 Sept. 1964. Unpublished Manuscript. *Donald Murray Collection*. The Milne Special Collections and Archives, University of New Hampshire, Durham.

———. "Letter to Mr. Walter Holden." 25 May 1970. *Donald Murray Collection*. The Milne Special Collections and Archives, University of New Hampshire, Durham.

———. "Letter to Robert F. Hogan." 17 Nov. 1972. *Donald Murray Collection*. The Milne Special Collections and Archives, University of New Hampshire, Durham.

———. "Letter to Robert S. Ireland." 6 Jan. 1970. *Donald Murray Collection*. The Milne Special Collections and Archives, University of New Hampshire, Durham.

———. "The Listening Eye: Reflections on the Writing Conference." *College English*, vol. 41, no. 1, 1979, pp. 13–19.

———. *The Literature of Tomorrow: An Anthology of Student Fiction, Poetry, and Drama*. Houghton Mifflin Harcourt, 1990.

———. *The Lively Shadow: Living with the Death of a Child*. Ballentine, 2003.

———. "Memo from Don Murray to Jean Kennard." 24 Jan. 1979. *Donald Murray Collection*. The Milne Special Collections and Archives, University of New Hampshire, Durham.

———. "Memorandum to Herb Jaffe and Myself." 28 Jan. 1962. *Donald Murray Collection*. The Milne Special Collections and Archives, University of New Hampshire, Durham.

———. *My Twice-Lived Life: A Memoir*. Ballentine, 2001.

———. "NESDEC Summer Workshop in the Teaching of Writing." Undated.

———. "Not-So-Good Old Days." *The Concord Monitor*, 23 July 1979, p. 10.

———. "One Writer's Secrets." *College Composition and Communication*, vol. 37, no. 2, 1986, pp. 146–53.

———. "Our Students Will Write—If We Let Them." *North Carolina English Teacher*, 1977.

———. "The Past, Present, and Future Meet in Every Decision We Make." *The Boston Globe*, 10 Jan. 2006, p. C3.

———. Personal interview by the author. 20 Nov. 2002.

———. "Personal Reflection." Undated. *Donald Murray Collection*. The Milne Special Collections and Archives, University of New Hampshire, Durham.

———. "The Politics of Respect." *Freshman English News*, vol. 9, no. 3, 1981, pp. 1–3.

———. "A Preface on Rejection." *Writing on the Edge*, vol. 5, no. 2, 1994, pp. 29–30.

———. "Preliminary Memorandum on Project to Improve the Teaching of Composition in Secondary Schools." 26 Sept. 1965. *Donald Murray Collection.* The Milne Special Collections and Archives, University of New Hampshire, Durham.

———. "Professional Reflection." 19 Jan. 1971. *Donald Murray Collection.* The Milne Special Collections and Archives, University of New Hampshire, Durham.

———. "Pushing the Edge." *Writing on the Edge*, vol. 5, no. 2, 1994, pp. 29–41.

———. "Reading What I Haven't Written." *New England Reading Association Journal*, vol. 40, no. 1, 2004, pp. 8–9.

———. "Reading While Writing." *Only Connect: Uniting Reading and Writing*, edited by Thomas Newkirk, Boynton/Cook, 1986, pp. 241–54.

———. "REFLECTIONS: The Child as Informer." *Language Arts*, vol. 57, no. 5, 1980, pp. 483–93.

———. "Rehearsing Rehearsing." *Rhetoric Review*, vol. 5, no. 1, 1986, pp. 50–56.

———. "Report on First Semester." 20 Jan. 1964. *Donald Murray Collection.* The Milne Special Collections and Archives, University of New Hampshire, Durham.

———. "Report on the Second Semester." 26 May 1964. *Donald Murray Collection.* The Milne Special Collections and Archives, University of New Hampshire, Durham.

———. "Sabbatical Report." 16 Sept. 1970. *Donald Murray Collection.* The Milne Special Collections and Archives, University of New Hampshire, Durham.

———. "Sabbatical report for Semester II, 1977–78 and summer 1978." 28 Aug. 1978. *Donald Murray Collection.* The Milne Special Collections and Archives, University of New Hampshire, Durham.

———. "Syllabus and Registration Form." Undated. *Donald Murray Collection.* The Milne Special Collections and Archives, University of New Hampshire, Durham.

———. "Teach the Motivating Force of Revision." *English Journal*, vol. 67, no. 7, 1978, pp. 56–60.

———. "Teach Writing as a Process Not Product." *The Leaflet*, vol. 71, no. 4, 1972, pp. 11–14.

———. "The Teaching Craft: Telling, Listening, Revealing." *English Education*, vol. 14, no. 1, 1982, pp. 56–60.

———. "Teaching the Other Self: The Writers' First Reader." *College Composition and Communication*, vol. 33, no. 2, 1982, pp. 140–47.

———. "Tricks of the Trade." *Notes in the Margins*, Stanford University, Fall 1993.

———. "What Can You Say Besides AWK?" *California English Journal*, vol. 9, no. 4, 1973, pp. 22–28.

———. "Why Teach Writing—and How?" *The English Journal*, vol. 62, no. 9, 1973, pp. 1234–37.

———. "Write Before Writing." *College Composition and Communication*, vol. 29, no. 4, 1978, pp. 375–81.

———. "Write Research to Be Read." *Language Arts*, vol. 59, no. 7, 1982, pp. 760- 68.

———. *A Writer Teaches Writing: A Practical Method of Teaching Composition.* Houghton Mifflin, 1968.

———. *A Writer Teaches Writing*, 2nd ed. Houghton Mifflin, 1985.

———. *A Writer Teaches Writing*, 2nd rev. ed. Heinle, 2004.

———. "Writing and Teaching for Surprise." *College English*, vol. 46, no. 1, 1984, pp. 1–7.

———. "Writing as Process: How Writing Finds its Own Meaning." *Eight Approaches to Teaching Composition*, edited by Timothy R. Donovan and Ben W. McClelland, NCTE, 1980, pp. 3–20.

———. "Your Elementary Pupil and the Writer's Cycle of Craft." *Connecticut English Journal*, vol. 2, no. 1, 1969, pp. 3–10.

Murray, Donald, and Les Fisher. "Memo to the Council for Educational Innovation." 26 Feb. 1970. *Donald Murray Collection*. The Milne Special Collections and Archives, University of New Hampshire, Durham.

———. "Perhaps the Professor Should Cut Class." *College English*, vol. 35, no. 2, 1973, pp. 169–73.

Myers, D. G. *The Elephants Teach: Creative Writing Since 1880*. Prentice Hall, 1993.

Nern, Michael G. *Donald Morison Murray's Contribution to the Teaching of Writing: An Investigation and an Application of His Teaching Ideas*. 1986. Ohio University, M.A. thesis.

New Directions in Composition Scholarship, 10–12 Oct. 1986. "Conference Program." *Donald Murray Collection*. The Milne Special Collections and Archives, University of New Hampshire, Durham.

Newkirk, Thomas. "Donald Murray and the 'Other Self.'" *Writing on the Edge*, vol. 19, no. 1 (Fall 2008), pp. 47–52.

———. "Locating Freshman English." *Nuts and Bolts: A Practical Guide to Teaching College Composition*, edited by Thomas Newkirk, Boynton/Cook, 1993, pp. 1–15.

———. "Lunch at the Nighthawk: Or Kinneavy Moves His Office." *Composition's Roots in English Education*, edited by Patricia Lambert Stock, Heinemann, 2011, pp. 61–71.

———. "Re: Greetings and Questions." Email to the author. 6 Dec. 2022.

———. "Why Donald Graves Matters—A Personal Recollection." *Children Want to Write: Donald Graves and the Revolution in Children's Writing*, edited by Thomas Newkirk and Penny Kittle, Heinemann, 2013, pp. 1–15.

Newkirk, Thomas, and Lisa C. Miller, editors. *The Essential Don Murray: Lessons from America's Greatest Writing Teacher*. Boynton/Cook Publishers, 2009.

North, Stephen. *The Making of Knowledge in Composition: Portrait of an Emerging Field*. Boynton/Cook Publishers, 1987.

Palmeri, Jason. *Remixing Composition: A History of Multimodal Writing Pedagogy*. Southern Illinois UP, 2012.

Peary, Alexandria. "The Hidden Ethos Inside Process Pedagogy." *Pedagogy*, vol. 14, no. 2, 2014, pp. 289–315.

Perl, Sondra. "Writing Process: A Shining Moment." *Landmark Essays on Writing Process*, edited by Sondra Perl, Routledge, 1994, pp. 1–22.

Pasternak, Donna L., et al. *Secondary English Teacher Education in the United States*. Bloomsbury, 2018.

Phillips Burns, Donna, et al. "College Composition and Communication: Chronicling a Discipline's Genesis." *College Composition and Communication*, vol. 44, no. 4, 1993, pp. 443–65.

"Proposal for a Doctor of Philosophy Degree in Education: Reading and Writing Instruction to be offered by the Department of Education University of New Hampshire Durham." 23 Apr. 1982. *Donald Murray Collection*. The Milne Special Collections and Archives, University of New Hampshire, Durham.

Qualley, Donna. "Murray and the Process of Internal Revision: A Think Piece." *Writing on the Edge*, vol. 19, no. 1, 2008, pp. 31–39.

Raymond, James C. "Review." *College Composition and Communication*, vol. 34, no. 2, 1983, pp. 228–30

Reigstad, Thomas. *Conferencing Practices of Professional Writers: Ten Case Studies*. 1980. State University of New York at Buffalo, Ph.D. dissertation.

Relating Reading and Writing in the College Years, 12–14 Oct. 1984. "Conference Brochure." *Donald Murray Collection*. The Milne Special Collections and Archives, University of New Hampshire, Durham.

Romano, Tom. "The Living Legacy of Donald Murray." *English Journal*, vol. 89, no. 3, 2000, pp. 74–79.

Root, Robert. "Donald Murray Remembered." *Writing on the Edge*, vol. 17, no. 2, 2007, pp. 10–29.

Rose, Mike. *Lives on the Boundary: A Moving Account of the Struggles and Achievements of America's Educationally Underprepared*. Penguin, 1989.

Routman, Regie. "Donald Graves: Outstanding Educator in the Language Arts." *Language Arts*, vol. 72, no. 7, 1995, pp. 518–25.

Russell, David R. "Romantics on Writing: Liberal Culture and the Abolition of Composition Courses." *Rhetoric Review*, vol. 6, no. 2, 1988, pp. 132–48.

Scanlon, Chip. "A Conversation About the Writing Craft with Don Murray. Writers@ Work: A Process Approach." Undated. *Donald Murray Collection*. The Milne Special Collections and Archives, University of New Hampshire, Durham.

Scudder, Harold H. "A Functional English Course." *The Journal of Higher Education*, vol. 11, no. 8, 1940, pp. 412–17.

Scudder, Harold H., and Robert G. Webster. "The New Hampshire Plan for Freshman English." *College English*, vol. 2, no. 5, 1941, pp. 492–98.

Sheils, Merrill. "Why Johnny Can't Write." *Newsweek*. 8 Dec. 1975, p. 58.

Smit, David W. *The End of Composition Studies*. Southern Illinois UP, 2007.

Smith, Jeanne Jacoby. "Anatomy of a High School Dropout." *World and I*, vol. 13, no. 7, 1998, pp. 306–19.

Steinberg, Erwin R. "Needed Research in The Teaching of College English." *College English* vol. 24 no. 2, 1962, pp. 149–52.

Stewart, Thomas J. "Aloneness and the Complicated Selves of Donald M. Murray." *Composition Studies*, vol. 39, no. 2, 2011, pp. 45–60.

Stock, David. "Who Was Warren Taylor?: A Microhistorical Footnote to James A Berlin's Rhetoric and Reality." *Microhistories of Composition*, edited by Bruce McComiskey, Utah State UP, 2016, pp. 192–216.

Stock, Patricia Lambert, editor. *Composition's Roots in English Education.* Heinemann, 2011.

———. "Introduction: The Intertwined Roots of English Education and Composition Studies." Lambert Stock, pp. 125.

Sunstein, Bonnie S. "A Stand in Time and Place: New Hampshire and the Teaching of Writing." *Composition's Roots in English Education,* edited by Patricia Lambert Stock, Heinemann, 2011, pp. 105–23.

Teaching Freshman English at the University of New Hampshire. Undated.

Tirabassi, Katherine E. *Revisiting the Current-Traditional Era: Innovations in Writing Instruction at the University of New Hampshire, 1940–1949.* 2007. University of New Hampshire, Ph.D. dissertation.

Tobin, Lad. "Donald Murray: An Appreciation." *College Composition and Communication,* vol. 58, no. 4, 2007, pp. 546–49.

"Toward Unity Through Diversity: Report of the University-Wide Educational Policies Committee." 15 Feb. 1967. *Donald Murray Collection.* The Milne Special Collections and Archives, University of New Hampshire, Durham.

Towle, Carroll S., and Robert G. Webster. *An Anthology: The University of New Hampshire.* UNH Press, 1941.

University of New Hampshire. *Bulletin of the University of New Hampshire Catalog Issue for 1925–1926.* University of New Hampshire, 1925.

University of New Hampshire. *Bulletin of the University of New Hampshire Catalog Issue for 1928–1929. University of New Hampshire, 1928.*

University of New Hampshire. *Bulletin of the University of New Hampshire Catalog Issue for 1935–1936.* University of New Hampshire, 1935.

University of New Hampshire. *Bulletin of the University of New Hampshire Catalog Issue for 1942–1943.* University of New Hampshire, 1942.

University of New Hampshire. *Bulletin of the University of New Hampshire Catalog Issue for 1945–1946.* University of New Hampshire, 1945.

University of New Hampshire. *Bulletin of the University of New Hampshire Catalog Issue for 1964–1965.* University of New Hampshire, 1964.

University of New Hampshire. *Bulletin of the University of New Hampshire Catalog Issue for 1966–1967.* University of New Hampshire, 1967.

University of New Hampshire. *Bulletin of the University of New Hampshire Catalog Issue for 1967–1968.* University of New Hampshire, 1967.

University of New Hampshire. *Bulletin of the University of New Hampshire Catalog Issue for 1968–1969.* University of New Hampshire, 1968.

University of New Hampshire. *Bulletin of the University of New Hampshire Catalog Issue for 1969–1970.* University of New Hampshire, 1969.

Varnum, Robin. "From Crisis to Crisis: The Evolution Toward Higher Standards of Literacy in the United States." *Rhetoric Society Quarterly,* vol. 16, no. 3, 1986, pp. 145–65.

Villanueva, Victor. *Bootstraps: From an American Academic of Color.* National Council of Teachers of English, 1993.

Voss, Ralph F. "Janet Emig's The Composing Processes of Twelfth Graders: A Reassessment." *College Composition and Communication,* vol. 34, no. 3, 1983, pp. 278–83.

Welsch, Kathleen A. "Review: History as Complex Storytelling." *College Composition and Communication*, vol. 50, no. 1, 1998, pp. 116–22.

Williams, Bronwyn. "Dancing With Don: Or, Waltzing With 'Expressivism.'" *Enculturation*, 11, 2011. https://www.enculturation.net/dancing-with-don.

Wlodkowski, Raymond J., and Margery B. Ginsberg. *Enhancing Adult Motivation to Learn: A Comprehensive Guide for Teaching All Adults*, 4th ed. Jossey-Bass, 2017.

Yagelski, Robert P. "'Radical to Many in the Educational Establishment': The Writing Process Movement After the Hurricanes." *College English*, vol. 68, no. 5, 2006, pp. 531–44.

Young, Ross. *What Is It "Writing for Pleasure" Teachers Do That Makes the Difference?* The Goldsmiths' Company/The University of Sussex, 2019, https://files.eric.ed.gov/fulltext/ED598609.pdf.

Zebroski, James Thomas. "Hidden From History: English Education and the Multiple Origins of Contemporary Composition, 1960–2000." *Composition's Roots in English Education*, edited by Patricia Lambert Stock, Heinemann, 2011, pp. 26–50.

Zirinsky, Driek. "An Interview with Donald Murray: 'Mucking Around in Language I Save My Soul.'" *Writing on the Edge*, vol. 4, no. 2, 1993, pp. 11–23.

Zugnoni, Michele N. *Encouraging Empowerment Through Expression: Creation of a Self-reflective Writing Group for First-generation College Students*. 2019. University of California, Davis, Ph.D. dissertation.